THE ELECTRIC TOILET
VIRGIN DEATH LOTTERY

Thomas Byrne is a fledgling genius and straight out of school. **Thomas Cassidy** is a writer, former teacher, and entrepreneur. Former Vice-Principal of Paddington Academy, he founded the CILCUS English Centre in Hong Kong. This is their first book.

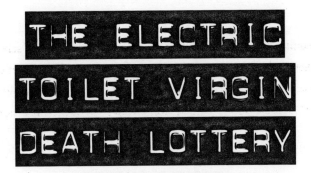

THE ELECTRIC
TOILET VIRGIN
DEATH LOTTERY

and Other Outrageous
Logic Problems

Thomas Byrne and Tom Cassidy

ONEWORLD

OXFORD

A Oneworld Paperback Original

Published by Oneworld Publications 2009

Copyright © Thomas Byrne and Tom Cassidy 2009

The right of Thomas Byrne and Tom Cassidy to be identified as
the Authors of this work has been asserted by them
in accordance with the Copyright, Designs and Patents Act 1988

All scenarios, whether they feature real people or fictional
characters, are fictional and have not been
approved by the real people or the originators or
owners of the fictional characters

All rights reserved
Copyright under Berne Convention
A CIP record for this title is available
from the British Library

ISBN 978–1–85168–692–6

Typeset by Jayvee, Trivandrum, India
Cover illustrations by Scott Garrett
Cover design by www.fatfacedesign.com
Printed and bound in Great Britain by the CPI Group

Oneworld Publications
185 Banbury Road
Oxford OX2 7AR
England
www.oneworld-publications.com

To Peter Cassidy, who lives in heaven now.
Thanks for starting this all off big fella,
it's a privilege to be your son.

and

Bernard A. Byrne and Roy D.J. Worrall —
wonderful Grandfathers

CONTENTS

ACKNOWLEDGEMENTS

From Thomas Byrne

Thanks to Matt for 'writing all the funny bits' and to Sophie for 'being the best girlfriend ever'. Thanks to Mike for his ideas and support, even though he wouldn't let us call Darwin a ..., and thanks to Mum, Dad, Ben, Jo and everyone who's helped along the way. Finally, thanks and congratulations to Tom for walking this path with me and doing some 'writing' and stuff.

From Tom Cassidy

Thanks to my amazing wife Cindy, my problem-solving genius children: Henry, Toby, Eddie, Maddison and Gabriel; my wonderful mum for being so supportive; Dominic, William and David, for talking about films a lot; and Sarah. And finally to all of those we had so much fun with along the problem-solving journey: Chris, Dafs, Ben, Matt, The Dribbler, Craig and Darth.

Over the next pages you will discover a wonderful selection of logicalistic conundrums. The problems are brilliant, and even the most cunning amongst you will struggle to solve all of them. However this mighty opus is far more than a mere repository of logic. For coiled around, entwined within and interlaced throughout are a group of characters so real, so remarkable, that you'll struggle to do anything but embrace them: there's Erik Van Basten – an evil criminal genius cum logician extraordinaire; the loveably incompetent Italian da Vinci twin, Manchesterano; Jemima the daft environmentalist; and a plethora of supporting characters. On top of this: rivalry, betrayal, death, surprise, intrigue, more death/ imminent death/death reloaded/double death and even a chance to take home some cash* …

You're in for a treat.

The problems

The problems you are soon to experience all have specific and elegant solutions. Although it's possible in some cases to arrive at the answer by throwing enough typewriters at Shakespeare's monkey, there will always be an easier and infinitely smarter way.

* See back page for competition details.

The solutions are clever, counter-intuitive and surprising and there are no trick questions. The solutions will leave you thinking, 'wow, that's so clever', and often after days spent ruminating, 'oh, that's so obvious'.

When it comes to difficulty, most of the problems are hard. However, by 'hard' we do not mean a complex solution involving π, $+$, arcsin and other crazy maths symbols running to several pages. They are 'hard' because the answers are, as mentioned above, counter-intuitive, surprising and most importantly, clever. Each problem has a hardness rating in the bottom corner to give you an idea of what you're getting yourself into and to allow you to prepare yourself mentally for what lies ahead.

Rating	Description
★	The problems of the novice, yet by no means a mere cuddling of the cerebrum. Persevere and the answers will come soon enough.
★★	Starting to get trickier. These problems will challenge, but after a while will leave you wanting more.
★★★	Palms sweaty, walls closing in, still no closer to that elusive solution. But you're going to make it; hang in there and it will come to you.

Only the professional problem-solver should open their mind to this level of logic and cunning. Known side effects include but are not limited to: skin discolouration, prickly rash, diabetes and paralysis.

 This level of problem is psychological suicide. It will leave you huddled in a dark corner, endlessly reciting the tortuous problem and cursing the day you ever bought this book.
You have been warned.

Guidance and help

The problems are, by their very nature, problematic and as such you should not expect anything close to an immediate solution. Problems will rarely be solved without a number of hours of solid pondering, which will often result in solutions taking days to emerge. While each solution will be different and independent of all others, there is a general approach that can be applied to all the problems when searching for illumination.

You should always, always begin by listing all the information the problem contains. This is slightly easier said than done, given the extensive use of rhetoric, allegory, plot twists and cliff hangers, but it must be done all the same. We've started this process for you with a Key Facts summary at the end of each problem, but there will always be more information lurking within the problem itself. When it comes to solutions, there are no red herrings, blue fruit baskets or misleading facts but there are often clues in the specific words chosen, so pay attention.

Just as important as determining what you do know, is realising what you *do not* know: challenge your assumptions. Assumptions generally mess everything up and you can avoid hours of wasted rumination by dealing with them straight off.

Take for instance the phrase: Someone 'fell out of a twenty storey building'. The immediate assumption is that they fell from the twentieth storey; however it does not say that at all! They could just have easily have fallen from the ground floor.

Solving the thing

Once you have determined what you do and do not know, you can set about trying to solve the problem. Here are a few techniques:

1. Extremes: Try reducing the problem to its simplest case, or exaggerating it to its upper limit. For example, if a problem involves 100 of something, try it out with one instead.
2. Reversal: Reverse the problem, look at it upside down and work backwards. If time is involved, for example, often the solution will be found by starting at the last day/minute/hour and working backwards instead of starting at the beginning and working forwards.

3. Counter-intuition: Often the most counter-intuitive thing will be exactly the right course of action. What at first glance might worsen the situation might be just the thing you need to do. For example, if you're stuck to the floor with glue on your shoes, try nailing your hands to the ceiling as well.

4. Symmetry: Problems are often symmetrical. For example if there are three options and two of them are reflections of each other, the correct solution must be the third option since it is unique.

The above techniques will certainly assist you in your journey, but leaps of genius will frequently be required. Therefore we have provided additional assistance for if and when you do get stuck: every problem has a selection of hints at the back of the book to guide you along the path to discovery.

The hints are incremental and each represent one step along the way to solving the problem. If, after a good lot of thinking, you are still stuck, look at the first hint before returning to the problem for another good lot of thinking. Go through the different techniques again and think further. If still stuck, move on to the next hint. Same procedure for the rest of the hints. There is no greater feeling than having worked out a problem yourself. It is pure ecstasy. What we're getting at is if you're alive and still possess brain function, *avoid looking at the answers*!

One last thing . . .

So you can see how well you're doing as you progress through the book we've provided a selection of rankings, to cover all variety of problem-solving mammals.

Hints required	How good you are compared to ...			
	Kitchen utensils	**Dates**	**Strokes**	**Star Wars characters**
0	Very sharp knife	Christmas Day	Stroke of genius	The Emperor
1	Sharp knife	Birthday	Stroke of luck	Darth Vader
2	Knife	Pay day	Breast stroke	Count Dooku
3	Blunt knife	14 May	Heat stroke	Jabba
4	Ladle	End of days	Ischemic stroke	Jar Jar

Finally, one of the best pieces of advice I was ever given was by my piano teacher Mrs Joyce Clarke (RIP). She said: 'Cut your fingernails every six days because once a week is just a bit too long.'

More relevantly she said, 'Go from the known to the unknown.' Keep that in mind and you shouldn't go too far wrong.

So, use the force, magic rings, your utmost ninja skills – whatever you can – and let's get cracking ...

PART I

Warm-ups with Erik Van Basten

We have a treat for you all — a series of warm-up problems narrated by basically the best character in the book; certainly the most cunning and evil, and without question the most fiendish. 'Who is this man Erik Van Basten?' I hear you cry. Well, we shall tell you:

From humble beginnings as a foetus, Erik developed at a devilish rate and grew naturally into a life of subversive genius. He was branded a 'difficult' child, largely due to his penchant for burning his teachers, and he was summarily expelled from every institution he attended. In spite of this, his native guile was so well developed that he managed to get accepted to read Treachery and Hard Sums at the world renowned Oxbridge University. Leaving with a first class degree, Erik turned his artistry to the music business and joined The Boomtown Rats on keyboards. (That's Erik doing the tasty piano intro to 'I Don't Like Mondays'.)

Unfortunately, Bob Geldof's burgeoning forays into mainstream pop and charity work frustrated Erik's post-punk-world-domination plans and he soon left the music industry. Intrigued by the corrupting potency of politics he formed the UN but that turned out to be really merde. Vraiment merde. Finally settling down to fulfil his true vocation, he began creating his very own criminal empire. As such Van Basten Corp. (VBC) was formed.

By the early 1990s, VBC had become a world leader in fraudulence and when Erik masterminded the theft of Wales for six months his position was sealed as the foremost evil genius this book had ever seen.

We reckon.

Anyway, what Erik's going to be doing in this chapter is relating some jolly japes from his past to tune you in to the subsequent madness. These warm-ups will flex your mental gymnastics and get you frothing for the problems you're about to encounter. It will also help you get an early indication as to whether you will be soaring like an Einstein or sinking like a Bush ...

Welcome Erik, the stage is yours ...

1

Wilkommen Freunds! I was at this gathering the other day and I stumbled across a magnificent problem for you all. It was a party celebrating thirty-five years since the invention of the Rubik's cube and the most amazing do had been laid on by Dr Rubik. Everyone was there: Picasso had done the displays, Ice Cube did the music and it all took place in Cuba. Brilliant.

The highlight of the evening was the cake: it was as big as a sofa and in the shape of a Rubik's cube!

Apart from being a metre tall it was a pretty simple sponge cake and as luck would have it, I'd brought with me my 'enormous-cake-cutting-device'. Hence it fell to me to share the cake amongst the guests. Coincidentally there were exactly twenty-seven guests at the party, each needing an equal share, and so I needed to end up with twenty-seven little cube-shaped pieces at the end of all the cutting.

1. What's the least number of cuts with which I could achieve the objective?

When I got home that evening I thought to myself that if only I'd also taken with me my 'enormous-cake-piece-manoeuvring-device' I would have been able to rearrange the pieces after each cut and surely saved myself some cuts.

2. Was I right? And why?

Key facts

- One large cake in the shape of a $3 \times 3 \times 3$ cube.
- One cake-cutting device.

Challenge

1 Divide large cube into twenty-seven equal mini-cubes with fewest cuts.

2 Can it be done with fewer cuts if you're able to move the pieces around after each cut?

Q1 ★

Q2 ★ ★

2

Once a year, teams representing all the various alien races in the Empire rock up to the Reading Hexagon for the annual Star Wars convention. Somehow Van Basten Corp. always gets roped into sponsoring Homo-Sapiens. There are several really cool competitions of course, but the one I always get most excited about is the intergalactic Speed Croquet championship.

The championship format is that of a simple knockout tournament and since there's always quite a few teams competing there's a veritable bundle of matches taking place.

Last year teams from 4,619 civilisations turned up to compete and one of my jobs was to organise the match schedule.

So basically I needed to know how many matches (byes don't count as matches) there were going to be. What is the quickest way to do that?

You'll love it by the way — ist ein corker.

Key facts

- 4,619 teams.
- Simple knockout tournament.

Challenge

How many matches are needed in total?

3

OUTBREAK IN THE MURJ

A couple of months ago there was an outbreak of a mutant strain of the rabies virus in Murjrakhistan. The virus was so deadly that the death toll was doubling every day and, based on population figures, the World Heath Organisation predicted that within thirty days the whole country would succumb.

Based on that prediction, how many days did it take for 25% of the population to die?

Key facts

- Death rate doubles each day.
- Takes thirty days for whole country to die.

Challenge

How many days until 25% of the population had died?

4

This one's a classic and it'll certainly have you checking your bills carefully next time you go to a restaurant …

The other day I decided to take my two best mates, Boris Von Kampf and Sheldon the Shifter, out to dinner to celebrate them knowing me. We had a great time. It gets to settling up at the end of the meal and the bill comes to £25. None of us has change so we each contribute a £10 note to the pot and the waiter goes off with £30. A couple of minutes later he comes back with some change. He's a pretty smart guy and so he gives us each £1 back and then pockets the other £2 as a tip.

Now here's where it goes weird, Maths Van Basten style:

We all spent £9 so that's $3 \times £9 = £27$

The waiter pocketed £2 which gives $£27 + £2 = £29$

But we started with £30, so where did the other pound go? Hmmm. I told you it was a good one …

Key facts

- Look again, they're just above.

Challenge

Where did the missing pound go?

5

This one is a touch more tricky but it does respond to a little bit of careful logic and a smidgen of cunning ...

So I'm in 'Nam playing a game of Russian roulette just like in the film *Deer Hunter* – that stuff really happened y'know. It was brutal. I'm obviously trying to up my chances of winning, not least because the alternative is death but also because the alternative is death.

Here are the details: It turns out that my rather unlikely and somewhat anachronistic adversary is none other than Mel C from the Spice Girls! She's pretty rock so I'd better be on my best game. Using a standard six chamber revolver, Sporty puts two bullets into adjacent chambers, spins the gun and fires one off.

Nothing doing – she survives and passes the gun to me. I'm allowed to do whatever I like from the following three options:

1. Spin the barrel again and then shoot.
2. Shoot without doing anything to the barrel.
3. Open the revolver, take the bullets out, replace them in any positions, spin and shoot.

What's the best thing to do? Clearly in order to minimise the chances of diversifying my head.

Key facts

- Russian roulette with a six chamber revolver.
- Two bullets in adjacent chambers.
- Mel C shoots first and survives.

Challenge

To minimise his chances of dying, should Erik spin the barrel and shoot; just shoot; or reposition the bullets, spin and shoot?

6

Last year, I was at the doctors waiting to get some things checked out when in walks this enormous woman, and I really mean enormous. Maybe even ginormous.

Overhearing her talking to her companion I discover that she used to weigh the preposterous figure of 300 kg and that she, quite amazingly, was 99% fat. My interest piqued, I continue to eavesdrop and learn that three months ago she decided to have a stomach bypass operation and is now coming back to see how she's got on.

On her way out I hear her saying to a friend that he told her some devastating news: Even without ingesting any sustenance over the last three months she was gutted to be told she was still a whopping 98% fat.

Next in to see the Doctor, I was astonished to overhear him proclaiming the treatment a success. Then I thought about it. Hmm, maybe he was right – maybe dropping from

99% to 98% fat was a big deal.

So, how much weight did she actually lose?

Key facts

- Woman was originally 99% fat and weighed 300 kg.
- Now she is 98% fat.

Challenge

How much weight did she lose?

7

This problem is certainly pretty tricky; in fact, over the years, it has baffled and angered many self-proclaimed problem-solving geniuses. Stick with it though, think it through, and I predict you'll have the mustard to see the light.

As I have too much money, I like to splurge vast sums of it away by letting myself lose in casinos. At present my favourite gambling emporium is an up and coming Middle-Eastern themed casino in Las Vegas: Osama's Palace.

In the epitome of unlikelihood Osama's Palace was awarded the contract to host the US Republican Party's 2009 Annual Conference, and I just happened to be visiting at the time. In order to create a reckless gambling fervour among the attendees, the casino organised an event to tap into the Republican's two biggest weaknesses: guns and national security. The 'Where's Osama Rocket Launcher Game' was born.

The audience have all been given rocket launchers and (somewhat hopefully) been told to restrain themselves for the moment. On stage are three tank proof doors and hidden behind one of them is an uncannily real, life size, Madame Tussaud's wax replica of Osama himself. Concealed behind the other two doors stand waxwork models of two Republican legends: George W. Bush and Kermit the Frog.

It is explained to the audience that they are allowed to shoot at the person behind only one of the doors. The audience then vote as to which door they wish to open. The audience elect a door, but the host, instead of opening the chosen door, opens one of the other two doors to knowingly reveal George Bush to the audience! Once the cheers have died down the host explains to the audience that they now have a choice between the two remaining unopened doors: They can open their original choice of door or they can open the other door.

What should the audience do; which door should they then open in order to maximise the chance of being able to let loose their rockets and vanquish (smithereens style) the foreign fiend?

Key facts

- Three doors.
- Behind two are booby prizes (George and Kermit),

while behind the third stands everything the
Republicans desire (Osama).

- You choose a door.
- The host, who knows the location of the prize, opens
  one of the remaining two doors to reveal a booby
  prize.
- You are now given the choice of either opening your
  original door or switching to the other closed door.

Challenge

Which door should you choose? Does it even matter?

PART II

VBC – Are you the next apprentice?

The position of world-leading-evil-genius brings much publicity. Of course this increases the difficulty of covertly clandestine operations but, on the plus side, it has boosted the public image of the Van Basten Corporation. As such, the HR department receives more applicants, pro rata, than Bono. Most applicants are dismissed out of hand for being either too bibacious or too diabetic, yet some do advance to the gruelling test phases and your ability to manipulate your auntie's sock drawer has seen you do just that.

The other applicants and yourself are now to be subjected to various tests of ruthless cunning, strategic evil and sock counting. However, it is the continual assessment of that most important of all criminal qualities that will lead to an offer of employment: cold, hard logic.

Bon chance. Güten Lücken. Chicken Licken.

8

DIET PILL DISASTER

Van Basten Corp. makes tremendous profits from the sale of FeelGoodButtGone, an anti-depressant diet pill popular among big-boned American women. Infiltrators from the Size Acceptance Movement have broken into the VBC distribution centre in Bishop's Waltham, and contaminated one batch of the pills.

A somewhat vexed Erik VB has decided to use this unfortunate turn of events as the first test for you and the other budding applicants hoping to become Erik's newest agent of cunning. There are ten batches each containing one thousand pills. Erik informs you that the mass of a normal pill is 9 mg but the mass of a contaminated pill comes in slightly less at 8 mg.

The candidates are tasked with individually determining which of the batches is contaminated. Easy. There is a highly sensitive electronic balance available to the candidates, but due to the sheer volume of applicants (they're all shouting) each candidate is only allowed to use the balance once. Less easy.

Erik is watching, and is looking forward to personally eliminating those that fail to find the contaminated produce. How can you determine which of the ten batches contains the contaminated pills in only one weighing?

Key facts

- Ten batches of pills.
- Contaminated pills weigh 1 mg less than normal pills.
- Highly sensitive electronic balance.
- Only one weighing allowed.

Challenge

Identify the contaminated batch …

… and there are sharks in the lake.

9

SOMETHING FUNNY

Due to a sweet tooth that he's never managed to grow out of, the front to Erik's evil HQ in Luton is an M&Ms factory. While the majority of man-hours are focused on furthering the boundaries of the VBC empire, in order to maintain a successful facade as a confectionary consortium, a certain portion of resources must necessarily be assigned to the business of manufacturing sweets.

However, since only a small slice of corporate attention is being devoted to creating M&Ms, an awfully large number of packets fail to reach the standards demanded by the Van Basten QA department and Mister Erik is *pas de jolie*.

Although somewhat dischuffed, he realises that this disaster can be used as another opportunity to test the ingenuity of his aspiring apprentices and sets them the following challenge:

Each applicant is placed in a room with an unlimited supply of packets of these sub-standard sweets. While there are several ways a packet of M&Ms can fail the quality control measures, the samples given to the applicants are bags that each contain either too many or too few confectionary items. Apart from this, each packet, and the delicious contents, are equal in every way.

Ok, so it seems an unlikely scenario but this book is riddled with unlikely.

So Mr Van Basten tasks the applicants with discovering the weight of an individual M&M. The only restriction is that none of the packets may be opened since they're going to be eventually sold to raise money for the 'Widows of Evil Near-Geniuses' of which Erik is an active patron.

You still have access to the highly sensitive electronic balance from the previous test and for the sake of irony you are now allowed unlimited weighings.

How can you determine the weight (mass) of one single M&M without opening any of the packets? More importantly can you do it quicker than the other candidates and shimmy into EVB's good books?

Key facts

- Different packets, identical in all aspects but weight and number of M&Ms.
- Unlimited number of packets.
- Highly sensitive electronic balance.

- Unlimited weighings allowed.
- No packets to be opened.

Challenge

Determine the mass of a single M&M.

10

At face value this next test appears most trivial, as it involves nothing more than choosing an amount between £0 and £100. Luckily, that is not the case for it involves deep psychological reasoning and strategy. Apparently.

Each candidate still in the contest chooses an amount of money between £0 and £100, inclusive. These amounts are then entered into the most advanced computing device VBC possesses: a 'calculator'. This 'calculator' will then work out the average of all the amounts, and then divide this number by three to end up with an amount of money: £x. (I know x is a letter – it's kind of like algebra or something.)

The winning candidate is the one whose chosen amount was closest to £x. The winner(s), Erik explains, will receive hundreds of pounds as a bonus and passage to the next round. If more than one person chooses the winning number, then the bonus will be shared amongst them.

What amount should you choose?

Of course, like yourself, all other candidates are perfectly logical geniuses and as such will be thinking along the same lines as you.

Key facts

- Everyone selects an amount of money from £0 to £100.
- The total of all the chosen amounts is divided by the number of contestants to get the average.
- This answer is then divided by three to give x.
- Everyone is perfectly logical.

Challenge

Choose the amount closest to x.

II

DYNAMITE DISTRACTION

It turns out that the previous problem is not such a good discriminator as nearly everyone got it right. All the spoils were shared which means that everyone got as much out of it as the authors are getting in royalties for this book.

So we have now entered the fourth week of testing and things are certainly hotting up. Those candidates who have failed to live up to Mr VB's soaring expectations have been sent home. In a box. Those that have just about scraped acceptance have been sent to stand in the corner. In a box. And those select few that have managed to actually impress Erik are enjoying a game of 'bounce the grenade'.

However, the fun and frolics promptly end as Erik announces the latest challenge for the surviving candidates.

The problem with being a world renowned criminal genius, Van Basten begins, is that people are always trying to sabotage your masterfully conceived plans. One such example, he relates, is how a group of dolphin-loving-hippy-vegans broke in to the HQ and completely messed up the painstakingly arranged microdynamite stockpile. The microdynamite had previously been arranged in order from lightest to heaviest, as weight is a very convenient indicator of explosive power.

Each candidate is assigned a collection of random dynamite sticks and they are informed that the sticks all weigh somewhere between 1 g and 40 g. Their challenge is to calculate the weight of their assigned sticks. In order to weigh their sticks, each candidate is given an old fashioned set of scales – you know, where you put what you're weighing on one side and put small weights on the other side until it balances.

The catch, however, is that while each candidate has access to an unlimited supply of weights with which to weigh the dynamite, the winner of the challenge will be the person who requires the fewest weights.

NB: Each stick of dynamite weighs a whole number of grammes, i.e. 1 g, 34 g but not 14.34 g, 12.56 g etc.

NB 2: There is a lake.

NB 3: There are sharks in it.

Key facts

- A selection of dynamite sticks weighing between 1 g and 40 g.
- You have a set of old fashioned balance scales to help you.

Challenge

To be able to weigh every dynamite stick using the fewest weights.

12

The end of the application process has finally arrived. The ten most cunning and fiendishly logical candidates have secured their futures as part of the great Van Basten Empire and are all to be allocated positions within the corporation at the graduation ceremony.

As great luck would have it, you have managed to 'stumble' upon Erik's plan for the allotment of said positions. There are currently five openings for evil geniuses in the establishment of a new office in Southernmost Patagonia – pretty mountains, but poor job prospects, and five posts available in the Department for Evil Doings at the VBC HQ – amazing job prospects, company slide.

Reading further through Erik's notes, you uncover his plan for the allocation of these positions. Erik, the epitome of fairness, has designed a process that leaves the choice to pure chance:

In one jar, labelled 'HQ', he has placed five red M&Ms, and in another jar, labelled 'Patagonia,' he has placed five blue ones. His plan is to have candidates don blindfolds and in turn randomly select a jar from under a blanket. Once they have selected the jar, they then put their hand inside and pull out a sweet.

Red = HQ. Blue = Patagonia. As keen a skier as you are, you would rather share a hammock with Noel Edmonds than work with Patagonian alpaca herders.

It is only minutes until the allocation procedure begins. You didn't make it into the final ten without a modicum of manipulative brilliance and so you're certain you can manoeuvre things to ensure you are the first person to choose, but that still only leaves you a 50/50 chance of securing the job you desire.

The jars have been placed under a blanket by EVB ready for the procedure to begin. Thinking quickly, you decide to rearrange the sweets in order to maximise the probability of picking a red one just as you hear the rustle of keys by the door …

How should you rearrange the M&Ms in order to do this?

Key facts

- Two jars.
- Five blue and five red M&Ms.
- You first select a jar at random.

- Then you select a sweet from that jar — also at random.
- You cannot eat the M&Ms.

Challenge

Put the M&Ms into the jars to maximise the chance of getting a red M&M.

13

With their unfortunate colleagues en route to Patagonia, the lucky five staying at VBC HQ are all pumped and raring to get on. Erik, however, has one last game in mind. Generous to a fault, he has set aside £1,000 to be shared amongst the new employees as a congratulatory gift. Taken aback by his kindness the applicants each go to collect £200 for themselves, forgetting that things are never that simple where Erik is concerned. Erik has his own rules for the division of the laundered cash ...

Based upon their performance throughout the application process, the five best employees have been ranked from first to fifth. Due to your gargantuan skills you have been ranked highest.

Congratulations.

Erik explains that the first applicant in the hierarchy will propose how he thinks the money should be split. All applicants vote on the proposal, and it will only be passed if at least half of the applicants decide to go along with it. If less then half vote yes, I'm afraid you will be executed, and the process will be repeated with the second ranking applicant (Hairy Back Gary) proposing a split. Again if more than half agree, it will be passed, but if less than half agree then he who made the proposal will also be executed and it will pass to the third applicant to suggest a split, and so on …

What split should you propose to keep your life, as much cash as possible and Gary the Gorilla from getting his hairy mitts on the readies?

Key facts

- £1,000 to be shared out between five applicants.
- Applicants are ranked 1–5. You are the top ranker.
- You propose a split first.
- All five vote whether to accept the proposal.
- If at least half vote to accept the proposal – it happens. Otherwise you are executed. Seems harsh but that's our Erik!
- The next-highest ranking applicant proposes a split between the remaining applicants.
- And so on until a proposal is accepted.
- As before, the applicants are all perfectly rational.

Challenge

1 Avoid death.
2 Keep cash.
In that order.

PART III

Mayhem with Manchesterano

Not many people know this, but Leonardo da Vinci had a twin brother who was, in many respects, a lot smarter: Manchesterano. Unfortunately, Manchesterano da Vinci failed to live up to his early promise and ended up following a path of relative obscurity. Being relegated to the role of lesser sibling was a hard pill to swallow as Manny felt he really had the edge on Leo on almost everything apart from the science, art, music, ambidexterity, inventions and medicine.*

This brought about much fraternal bitterness and after a particularly vitriolic exchange with his increasingly famous

---

* and looks, tennis, personality and blood type.

brother, Manny vowed to out genius Leonardo. He had himself cryogenically frozen with the intention of becoming reactivated when his bro' was old and grey. Leonardo declined this new technology believing that it was 'largely unproven'.

Well, it turns out that Manchesterano overestimated the defrosting promise of the sixteenth century, and indeed the seventeenth, eighteenth and nineteenth. For only in the 1990s was he restored to his warm-blooded self ...

At present, Manchesterano – a little cold and with no one to impress – is a star on the rise. His post-defrosting academic thesis 'Balls to you, Leo' left him shunned by the scientific community, so he turned his attention to show business. Success followed and he's currently touring the globe with his celebrity-compere-pyro-variety-act. Let's catch up with him and see where he's plying his trade today ...

14

Celebrity sensation Manchesterano has been invited to visit his special brand of humour upon the world at that most prestigious event in the entertainment community: the Oscars.

Manny has an extensive entourage that assist him with his many death-defying tricks that all require a level of technical sophistication redolent of Genesis concerts. 'A tightly orchestrated spectacle involving explosives, fire, exploding fire, bangs, whizzes and Britney in a cake is sure to render me a global superstar', he muses.

To avoid press intrusion he splits his team of technical wizards into smaller groups to rehearse independently and sends them to three different cities: Vegas, San Diego and Los Angeles itself.

One thing that Manny is always consistent about is rotating his staff: to avoid them getting stale he never lets them know on exactly which team they are going to be in and this event, despite its magnitude, was no exception. So, he gives the following instructions.

His team of thirty illusionists are to turn up independently at Heathrow airport at random times during departure day and simply get on the first flight departing to any of the three destinations. It just so happens that there are an equal number of daily flights to all three destinations, and so Manny deduces that he will end up with three approximately equal teams at each location. Each team will be poised to perfect their individual segment of the Manchesterano Magic Show.

However, there is a slight problem …

Upon arriving in Hollywood boulevard to coordinate the operation, Manny is astonished to learn that his beautifully conceived plan has hit a snag: there are twenty-five people in Vegas, and only two in San Diego with a further three in LA itself.

What went wrong?

None of the staff have disobeyed his instructions and there were indeed an equal number of flights to each location but somehow twenty-five out of thirty people ended up in Vegas.

And no, they didn't decide to go gambling.

Key facts

- Three destinations.
- Equal number of daily flights to each destination.

- Staff arrive at random times throughout the day.
- Staff catch the first flight to any destination.
- Staff follow instructions precisely.
- The end result is not a 10:10:10 split but a 25:2:3 split.

Challenge

Find out how this could happen.

15

THE MOST EXPENSIVE DRINK IN THE WORLD?

Despite the preparatory issues, Manny pulled off the best Oscars ceremony in years and it is now time for the after party, and a glass or two of bubbly ...

In 1998, 2,000 bottles of Hiedsieck Champagne – the Diamant Bleu Vintage 1907 – were found by leopard sharks in the shipwreck of the Swedish freighter Jönköping in the Gulf of Finland. At $275,000 a bottle it's possibly the most expensive drink in the world, and Warren Buffet has decided to reward the film industry for 'lots of jolly good films' and bought all the bottles for the after party.

Just as Manchesterano is preparing to launch the debauchery, a note arrives from the troublesome Screenwriter's Guild saying that one of the bottles has been poisoned.

It gets worse – the poison is tasteless, odourless and its only symptom is sudden death kicking in after about forty-five minutes.

It's a pretty tricky dilemma, as the champagne is so expensive they really, really don't want to throw it away. But since no one can tell which bottle has been poisoned, it appears they may have no choice.

However, Manchesterano draws upon his entire bounty of genius and comes up with a cunning plan that will not only identify the poisoned bottle but do so in less than an hour so that the evening's revelry can continue with minimum disruption.

The plan involves using his own men as human guinea pigs and, while he is quite prepared to sacrifice a few of his entourage for the greater good, being a considerate boss he would prefer to keep his human losses to a minimum.

What's the lowest number of servants he needs to make sure he can test all 2,000 bottles within the timeframe?

Key facts

- 2,000 bottles of champagne.
- One of the bottles is poisoned.
- The poison takes forty-five minutes to have any effect.
- One-hour time limit.

Challenge

What is the lowest number of his retinue that Manny must place at risk in order to test all the bottles within the timeframe?

16

THE ELECTRIC TOILET VIRGIN DEATH LOTTERY

The constant bright beams of stardom have taken their toll and Manchesterano now fears that he may lose the many fans that were originally drawn to his 'brother trying to make a buck' attitude. Consequently, he has decided to return to his roots and the more *intimate* gig and so he's on his way to Huckleberry, USA.

It is a big day in the small Virginian town, for 100 years ago today their first flushing toilet arrived. The inhabitants have organised a day of celebrations, and Manchesterano has come to delight the crowd. After hours of exhibitions showcasing the latest in flush technology and the customary toilet-themed novelty displays, it is time for Manchesterano's eagerly anticipated finale: the electric toilet virgin death lottery.

A hundred toilets, one for each year of flush brilliance, have been lined up along main street and in front of each of them stands a choice Huckleberry virgin. However, unbeknownst to Huckleberry's inhabitants, and indeed the virgins, Manchesterano has secretly hooked each of the toilets up to the national grid. For fun.

Of course, communal sacrifice is not routinely considered PC, but let's not forget that Manchesterano is from a bygone age; an age when human life is considered entertainment's subordinate.

Anyway, Manchesterano fires a gun, and all 100 toilets become electrified. He shoots again, and every second toilet is switched off. On the third shot every third toilet is toggled, i.e. switched off if already electrified or switched on if not electrified. This toggling continues in a similar fashion: Every fourth toilet on the fourth shot, every fifth toilet on the fifth shot ... right up to the hundredth toilet on the hundredth shot.

After all this shooting, Manchesterano explains that all virgins are to sit on their respective toilets. It is fair to say that this really isn't what the Huckleberry inhabitants had in mind when they booked 'Manchesterano, the family orientated entertainer', but even so, a great hustle and bustle ensues as the inhabitants all rush to enter the lottery and hopefully win the cash prize by accurately guessing the correct number of virgins who will sit and never again stand.

Manchesterano gives the command and the virgins sit. It is a macabre affair and no mistake, but the question on everybody's lips is, 'How many virgins suffered the shock of their lives?'

Key facts

- 100 toilets and 100 shots.
- Raised toilet seat is electrified, lowered is harmless.
- On the first shot every toilet seat is raised.
- On the second shot every second toilet seat is raised.
- On the third shot every third toilet seat is toggled, i.e. raised if down or lowered if up.
- Process continues up to and including the hundredth shot.
- The virgins sit on their toilets.

Challenge

How many virgins are sacrificed?

17

TECHNOLOGY IS THE DEVIL'S FRUITCAKE

Ever since the electrocuted-virgins fiasco of Huckleberry, the demand for Manchesterano and his comedy-magic-variety act has all but disappeared. His career in tatters, Manchesterano has decided to go on a life affirming trek across the USA: find one's soul, bond with nature, kill a koala, etc.

Leaving LA behind him with nothing but a backpack, steely determination and a bag of nuts, he heads east and into the Mojave Desert. Having grown up amongst the olive trees and vineyards of sun dappled Tuscany, he is ill-prepared for the fierceness of the harsh desert and is rather quickly left dehydrated, confused and lost.

His loud hallucinations and vain attempts at a rain dance bring him to the attention of some passing tribesmen who decide to take poor Manny back to their village, hidden deep within the desert. Provided with something to drink and a place to rest, Manny recovers from his dehydrated tribulations. With nothing waiting for him in the outside world, he decides to stay in the village to learn about their primitive ways and hopefully find solace within himself.

As the weeks pass, he soon discovers that the tribe has three strict rules. Firstly, technology is considered the Devil's love child and is therefore strictly forbidden. Secondly, in an interesting system of discipline, a man is only answerable to his wife, who, if she discovers her spouse breaking any tribal rules, must kill him that very day. Lastly, Manny learns that tribal members are completely forbidden to interfere with the lives of others and all conform to this rule diligently. The village is made up of exactly eighty couples.

As Manchesterano interacts more closely with the villagers, he learns that all eighty of the husbands have succumbed to the lure of modern technology and, contravening the tribe's most sacred rules, have each secretly bought themselves a mobile phone. Delving and gossiping further he discovers that all wives are aware of everything going on in the village other than their own partner's indiscretions.

Finally at peace with himself, Manchesterano decides it is time to be moving on. On his last night the villagers organise a party in his honour. Intoxicated and cheerful, Manchesterano lets slips that at least one of the husbands owns and is using a mobile phone.

As the party comes to a close, no one gives much thought to his revelation, after all, every wife knows of seventy-nine mobile phone wielding husbands so Manny divulged nothing they didn't already know.

The following day Manchesterano bids farewell and heads on his way.

What will happen?

Key facts

- Eighty couples in the village.
- Wives have perfect knowledge of everyone but their own husbands.
- Any wife learning her husband owns a mobile must kill him the same day.
- Manny tells all the wives that at least one of them has an errant husband.
- The wives are completely rational beings. As if.

Challenge

Find out what happens.

18

Blissfully unaware of the carnage in his wake, Manchesterano has returned to LA to search for a new job outside the cut throat world of big entertainment. What he lacks in credibility and credentials he makes up for in enthusiasm, and he soon manages to secure new employment. Erik Van Basten, always keen to try new things, has recently opened a taxidermy division at VBC and has decided to take Manny on as the company's chief animal hunter. In an unfortunate twist, the first animal he is tasked with capturing by Erik is the most elusive and cunning, penguin-bison hybrid of northernmost Greenland: the byguin.

After months of searching along the inhospitable, ice covered coast of the north of the country in his boat, the Sea Squirrel, a very cold Manchesterano has finally located a fine byguin specimen, sitting in the centre of a perfectly circular ice floe.

As instructed, at first sight of the animal Manny contacts Erik, such that by the time the Sea Squirrel reaches the edge of the ice Erik has already relocated his orbiting spy satellite to enjoy a live video feed of the action from his castle in Penzance.

Manny is on the point of venturing onto the ice, net in hand, when Erik stops him, informing him that the floe won't hold both his and the byguin's weight, but not to worry as Manchesterano will be able to capture the animal from the confines of his craft. Of course, shooting the specimen would not work since the bullet wound would result in an imperfect skin for the VBC Taxidermy stuffed animal display.

Instead, Erik conjects: since the Sea Squirrel's top speed is four times that of the byguin, Manny will always be able to capture the animal when it attempts to leave the ice in search of food. As long as Manny tracks the animal accurately whenever it makes a dash for the sea, he can always make it to the specific point of the byguin's departure first and will therefore easily capture the animal.

Since the ice floe is perfectly circular, the distance from the centre to the edge is, of course, a radius. The distance Manny would have to sail the Sea Squirrel is further than the distance the byguin has to travel because he has to go around the circular ice floe but it should never be more than half a circle unless he is a complete cretin. Therefore Manny has to travel half the circumference. Since the Sea Squirrel goes four times faster than the byguin moves on land, he should be able to nip comfortably around ahead of his prey.

Continuing, Van Basten explains that should the byguin make it to the edge of the ice sheet before Manny arrives, it will easily make its escape since its speed in water is hugely impressive. Plus it can swim underwater and isn't afraid of the shark ubiquity headache that plagues this tome.

Erik has some evil doing to see to, and has to leave the video link, but warns Manny that he better bag the byguin or he'll be shipped back to Huckleberry prontissimo. In a box: Van Basten style.

Manny sets out to wrap up this routine capture but much to his astonishment, and despite following his new boss's instructions to the letter, the byguin escapes from the edge of the ice and into the murky depths of the ocean. On hearing this Erik is furious, blaming the escape on Manchesterano's incompetence, and immediately fires him, returning him to a life of ex-comedic poverty.

Manchesterano, however, is certain he did nothing wrong. Can he for once leave his buffoonery behind him and prove to his family, his fans and, most importantly, himself that it was not actually his fault that there is no byguin to taxidermate?

As is the case with all boats in VBC's fleet, the Sea Squirrel can turn instantaneously and also boasts immediate acceleration from zero to top speed. Strangely, the same two attributes are shared by byguins.

Key facts

- The ice floe is 30 m across.
- The Sea Squirrel can move four times as fast as the byguin on land.
- The byguin in the sea is uncatchable.
- For simplicity you can take π as 3.14.
- The Sea Squirrel tracks the byguin such that it always moves to the point on the edge of the ice floe that the byguin is approaching.

Challenge

How does Manny in the Sea Squirrel fail to catch the byguin?

Or, if you prefer – how does the byguin elude Manchesterano?

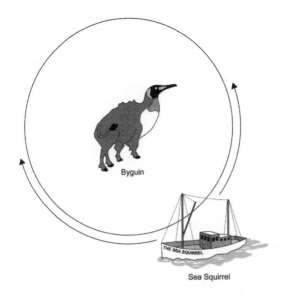

Figure 1 The byguin eludes the Sea Squirrel

PART IV

Jemima Planet and Friends

Jemima is a trouper, a super-trouper, shining like the sun; smiling, having fun and saving the world and all that. She spent many years working at Friends of the Earth but, in the end, decided that they were just a bunch of hippies who really didn't do anything useful other than eat dolphins on oil rigs or something like that. Consequently she decided to set up her own pre-neo-post-modern green activist group: Los Amigos del Soil. Accused of a breathtaking lack of originality by her fellow activists and shunned by the green media, she fled to Belize to build her own band of trepid eco-warriors ...

Fast forwarding to the present day ...

It has come to the attention of Los Amigos that the Van Basten M&M factory has been hiding much more than just the standard criminal array of pickpocketing, fraud and guttering; indeed a biochemical nuclear weapons facility operates within the premises. Accordingly, a quantity of weapons-grade, ebola ridden plutonium, large enough to power and/or kill a small horse, has been stockpiled. Los Amigos have decided to act, and it is time for *you* to join them in their first adventure.

Thus begin the exploits of Jemima Planet and Los Amigos del Soil ...

19

PREPARATION'S SECOND COUSIN ONCE REMOVED

While researching the mission, Jemima has been lucky enough to stumble upon an anonymous blog by one of Erik's disgruntled employees. Thinking that this may be a chink in the Van Basten armour, she uncovers the blogger's identity: Gaston le Pis.

When Erik chose one of his 'fancy new apprentices' to head up the VBC Bio Nuclear Programme, Gaston felt snubbed as he had been a loyal servant for many years. Receiving an email from Jemima he realises she is the perfect ally to help him bring down the nuclear operation and get the successor sacked so that he can swoop in, pick up the pieces and win back Erik's grateful touch.

Gaston decides to pass Jemima the secret information she needs to break into the plant. However there is a problem: ever since America stole the internet in 1991 the CIA have been able to intercept all electronic communications, so Gaston needs to secure his messages. For if any of the information he plans to give to Los Amigos fell into the hands of the CIA they would be able to bring the entire VBC operation to its knees, which would be bad. Very bad.

A little about encryption:

> All sensitive information sent through the internet is encrypted to prevent anyone reading it. To encrypt a piece of sensitive information, the sender and the intended receiver will both possess a specific encryption key. This is a very large prime number* of several hundred digits. In simple terms, the sender will firstly convert the information they wish to send into numerical form and then multiply it by this large prime number. This renders the information encrypted, and then the only way to decrypt the message is by possessing the large prime number it was multiplied by. (It can also be done using a very large computer, but takes a very, very long time: years, in fact.) Obviously, if the person you're trying to keep the information from has the encryption key themselves, i.e. the large prime number, they will be easily able to decrypt and read your sensitive message.

Gaston can encrypt the email, but anything easy enough for Jemima to decrypt, the CIA will be able to decrypt also.

* Only divisible by itself and 1, e.g. 13.

Therefore a really high level encryption method must be used. The conundrum is he can't just send Jemima the decryption key beforehand, because the CIA will then also have it and promptly discover the secrets themselves.

So how can Gaston pass the necessary information to Jemima without it falling into the hands of the CIA? As the only method of communication open to them is email, you can assume that the CIA will be aware of any plan that is concocted, so it had better be good.

What is it?

Key facts

- The only way Gaston can communicate with Jemima is via email.
- All unencrypted email will be intercepted and read by the CIA.
- This therefore prevents Gaston just sending Jemima the encryption key.

Challenge

How can Gaston and Jemima exchange these crucial emails without the CIA getting hold of the information?

20

'HOW I BECAME THE ONE THEY CALL THE VIKING'

With the crucial information that Jemima was sent by Gaston, our posse of intrepid activists have successfully broken into the Van Basten establishment to plunder plutonium, sally forth and strike a blow for soil bandits all over the world. However once inside the building you realise the security system to the lab is not quite what you expected ...

It turns out that Erik is a massive fan of rare 1970s Superfunk and access to the lab depends on switching multi-coloured lamps on and off in specific sequence, in time to 'Tear the Roof off the Sucker' by Parliament.

There are three lights: Red, Blue and Green and they shine directly onto the frequency-dependent unlocking system on the lab door. Somehow.

While Gaston has supplied you with this light-switching sequence, there is a snag: The lights are right next to the lab door and the switches are on the floor above, but there is no visual link between the control room and the lights. There are three switches in the control room, each one controlling a light but with no way of knowing which one, as there are no markings next to the switches. All the switches start in the 'Off' position. Due to the time constraints of a highly complex break-in like this, you only have time to make one trip to check out the lamps before running the sequence.

How can you determine which switch controls which light in order to run the sequence (R-B-G-B-R-G-B-G)? More importantly, how can you do it without funking things up?

Key Facts

- There is a control room with three switches – let's call them 1, 2 and 3.
- There are three different coloured lights that shine on the lab door – let's call them R, B, G.
- You do not know which switch controls which light.
- There is no visual link between the switches and the lamps.
- There is only time to make one dash to the lights and back.

Challenge

Identify which switch controls which light.

21

Somehow you manage to work out which switch controls which light and you run the sequence, enter the lab, locate the plutonium solution and escape with a 12 litre container filled to the brim with ebola ridden radiogenic liquid.

You are then immediately presented with your next challenge: Outside the pressure and temperature controls of the laboratory you must divide the plutonium mix into amounts of no more than 6 litres to avoid critical mass being achieved and instant meltdown. However you neglected, somewhat surprisingly considering the depth of planning required for this operation, to bring either a suitable container or a measuring device.

Fortunately you do have a couple of empty fizzy pop containers that you can sacrifice. Less fortunately, they are 8 litres and 5 litres in size.

Key facts

- You start with 12 litres of liquid plutonium in a 12 litre container.
- In addition you have an 8 litre and a 5 litre container.
- There are no volume markings on any container.
- There are very small, radioactive sharks in the plutonium. Nanosharks.

Challenge

To split the 12 litres of plutonium into two containers each containing 6 litres.

22

THE BRIDGE OVER THE RIVER SHARK

Having successfully divided the plutonium into safe transit volumes the party immediately discovers its latest challenge:

Standing between the group and their freedom is a deep mountain ravine, which can only be traversed via a rickety old rope bridge. Many of the bridge's wooden slats are missing and therefore it is impossible to cross safely without seeing where you are stepping.

Unfortunately it is night time, and so you will need a torch to guide you and there is only one torch in the group.

To further compound your woe, the bridge is weak and holds a maximum of two people at a time. Plus it's a long bridge, a bridge that snakes around the side of a mountain.

And as bad luck would have it, your exploits have been uncovered: a band of Erik's minions are only fifteen minutes behind you and are more than slightly vexed.

As if that's not enough, there are some restrictions on how long it takes your team to get across the bridge due to the equipment you are carrying:

- Jemima, known for mountain goat agility can zip across in only one minute.
- You're pretty nippy too but are carrying a lot of the supplies, so it's going to take you two minutes.
- Leon, who is carrying 6 litres of plutonium in a 12 litre container, can still move reasonably steadily so he'll make it across in only five minutes.
- Jean-Paul-Jean, with the smaller 8 litre container, cannot make it in less than eight minutes for fear of spilling his unlikely cargo.

How do you manage to get yourself and the other three in your team safely to the other side of the bridge in only fifteen minutes, so that you can burn down the bridge before the aggravated army of Van Basten is upon you?

Key facts

- You cannot cross the bridge without a torch.
- The bridge can only hold a maximum of two people at any one time.
- You have only one torch.
- You take different times to cross the bridge:

- Jemima – one minute;
- You – two minutes;
- Leon – five minutes;
- Jean-Paul-Jean – eight minutes.

Oh, and there are sharks in the river. Or tigers. No, I've got it – *very big* chickens.

Challenge

You have fifteen minutes to get all four of you across the bridge.

23

Having managed to get you all across safely, Jemima is feeling pretty pleased with herself until she spies the fiendish Van Basten crowd amassing on the other side of the bridge. They seem to have at least one torch each and they appear not to be burdened by either supplies or loosely covered plutonium containers. Jemima rightly surmises that they are going to be able to cross the bridge in one minute. She thinks of ways in which she can destroy the bridge: the ropes are too hard to cut through in the time; setting fire to them would also take too long for the ropes to burn through, so the only way of doing it is to blow the bridge and prevent the pursuing forces from crossing the gorge.

In anticipation of just this eventuality Jemima brought with her a highly complex chemical-composite bomb with enough explosive power to reduce the bridge, and indeed much of the mountain, to rubble.

Having attached it to one of the bridge struts she is just about to set it off when she has a revelation of brutal cunning. The best time to blow the bridge is not immediately, but rather when the Van Basten infidels are actually *on* the bridge. This would not only prevent her eco-bunnies from being captured but would serve the greater purpose of destroying many of the most evil Van Basten henchmen. Nice. So the ideal time to blow the bridge is at forty-five seconds – the whole platoon would have had time to get on the bridge but the fastest would still be several metres from safety at the time of explosion.

Alas, the highly technical bomb has no built in timing device, so therefore she has to calculate forty-five seconds. Unfortunately, in a rather wonderfully contrived juxtaposition of new and old, the only timing device she has with which to count forty-five seconds are two old-fashioned string fuses.* Much to her chagrin, she discovers that the fuses are each for sixty seconds. What's more, they are irregular burning fuses, which means that she can't get forty-five seconds by just cutting one down in size a bit.

How does she manage to get a forty-five-second period with these two fuses?

* By fuses we don't mean the built-in safety devices in electronic appliances, but the old-fashioned, Guy Fawkes type slow burning materials.

Key facts

- Two one-minute fuses.
- The fuses are irregular.
- You have matches.

Challenge

Time forty-five seconds.

PART V

Richard and Genghis

Asia. AD 1195. 4 March. Tea time.

Richard I — what a guy. Contrary to popular belief and modern cinema, he wasn't actually a lion, but just a man. Rumour has it though that he did once see a lion, but from seeing to being is quite a leap. Even though he wasn't a lion, and that certainly is a bit disappointing, he is still considered one of England's greatest kings. Anyway, he's been passing some time in the Middle East doing some crusading and what not, but is beginning to tire of it all.

Before he originally set out for the Holy Lands, he had created for himself a list of things he wanted to accomplish. Reviewing the list in Acre he realises there is, in fact, nothing left for him to do here:

- Take Jerusalem ✔
- Find Grail ✔
- Take some great holiday snaps ✔
- Swim with the Nazis ✔
- Eat dolphins ✔
- Invent electricity ✔

Therefore, he decides to head for home ...

24

BOIL FOR THREE MINUTES AND EAT WITH TOAST

Having decided to leave, Richard gathers up his knights, jumps aboard his ship and sets sail. Unfortunately, that really was the entirety of the preparations. The madcap manner in which the journey began has left Richard and his knights in the middle of an unknown ocean, heading in an unknown direction and generally in a bit of a kerfuffle. To further compound their woes, no one can find any navigation equipment on board: no maps, no compass, no GPS.

Fortunately, Merlin the Wise has been letting his marvellous mind run wild and has come up with a solution to their tribulation. He has, he explains, been watching the skies since they left port and by tracking the locations of the stars each night he has been able to determine their location. He assures Richard that, by continuing to use this method, he should be able to guide the ship home to England's pleasant shores.

They must continue in their current direction for exactly eleven hours, at which point they must turn due east and, following the new bearing, they will arrive in Portsmouth two weeks hence.

Before everyone starts celebrating, Merlin tempers their exuberance: due to the vast distance concerned, he explains, if the ship is turned even a few minutes too late or early, the bearing would be out by a few degrees, and in all likelihood ruin all hope of ever reaching home. Of course no one has a watch in order to keep track of time, but everything is not lost: fortunately, someone has found an eight-hour hourglass and a five-hour hourglass below deck.

While Merlin the Wise is undoubtedly wise, he has always struggled with numbers and, to be honest, is in fact dyscalculic. Therefore, Richard tasks you with discovering how the hourglasses can be used to measure exactly eleven hours. No pressure, but Richard promises to chop off your head if you fail to do so before the day is out.

And while the task in front of you is certainly tricky, escape is even less viable. You're in the middle of the sea and the nearest land is hundreds of miles away; you'd certainly die of dehydration before reaching safety, and, let's face it, you can't even swim. And you're wearing full battle armour, so you'll sink, and it's a full moon so the mermaids are out and up to their usual mischief. And, of course, it goes without saying that there are sharks in the sea.

Key facts

- You have an eight-hour and a five-hour hourglass.

Challenge

You need to measure eleven hours.

25

Congratulations: you did a brilliant job solving the problem with the hourglasses. Your comrades, crew and King were all thoroughly impressed. Unfortunately, Merlin's initial astronomical observations were exactly wrong and through an unfavourable combination of poor winds, strange weather and some sort of time-travelling-teleportation-device, the ship has arrived in outermost Mongolia. Making matters worse, the scouts of the great Mongol madman, Genghis Khan, have spotted you. His army is surely not far behind.

Disembarking, Richard sets about preparing his troops for battle. In a stroke of good fortune, the point at which the ship beached was in fact atop a mountain, so our verbicidal King can see the troops of Genghis preparing in the distance. Now, while Richard is famed for his fearlessness in battle, the sense of invincibility he inspired in his men and his wonderful Scottish accent, what is often forgotten is that he was actually a brilliant mathematician and possessed an unrivalled understanding of all things trigonometricalistic. Using this skill, Richard determines that the opposition forces are exactly twenty miles away. In order to track their movements and hopefully learn their plans, Richard sends Merlin to scout ahead.

While a rather feeble astronomer, mathematician and, it must be said, magician, Merlin is a master of disguises and brilliant spy. Richard instructs him to ride directly towards the enemy camp, learn what he can and then return to Richard to recount all he has discovered. He will then immediately head back to the Mongols, before coming back to Richard, then back to the enemy, and so on … In a coincidence not unheard of in this book, the instant at which Merlin initially leaves Richard's camp, the opposing forces both start moving towards each other.

Merlin, travelling by himself upon a plutonium steed, moves at a constant speed of 30 mph. The Mongol army are also on horseback, and despite their heavy weaponry and kleptomania, are travelling at a respectable 11 mph. Richard and his knights, weighed down by armour and travelling on foot, are moving at a meagre 4 mph.

The question you must answer is how much plutonium Merlin's magic mount will have consumed by the time the two armies reach each other if she burns through the energy source at a rate of 1 g per mile travelled. Merlin is a master horse rider and through gentle whisperings and encouragement is able to get out of his horse both immediate acceleration and instant turn arounds. In fact, his horse might actually be a byguin.

Key facts

- Two armies twenty miles apart begin moving towards each other.
- Richard's army travels at 4 mph.
- Genghis's army travels at 11 mph.
- Merlin leaves Richard's army at the instant both armies start to move, and travels backwards and forwards between the armies until they meet. He travels at 30 mph.

Challenge

Find out how far Merlin travels and therefore how much plutonium his radioactive steed has exhausted.

26

Even though Merlin provided Richard with almost perfect knowledge of the Mongol's plan, the battle lasted less than three minutes. Badly outnumbered, it was never going to be one for Churchill's History of Britain; Richard and his Knights were rounded up, thrown into prison and told to prepare for a fate marginally worse than death.

Despite his men's calls for an immediate mass execution of the foreign invaders, Genghis's fabled penchant for logic problems inspires him instead to offer his captives a problem. The solution to which will set them free, but failure will see them killed in a manner most horrid.

On hearing this, Richard, not yet impressed by the mental capacities of these barbarians, immediately accepts the challenge. Genghis rubs his hands together and sets about preparing for the evening of his life: logic, death and sharks – amazing. Richard and his knights are all blindfolded and have hats placed on their heads. Genghis sits them in a circle, tells them to be silent and explains what they've got themselves into:

> You are each wearing a hat, he explains. The hat is either red or blue; it is never yellow. Once your blindfolds are removed you will all be able to see the hat colour of your companions but you are forbidden to talk in any way, in code or otherwise, about the colour of any hat. The challenge I put to you, is for one of you to be able to stand up and correctly determine the colour of your hat. If you can do this, you will all be freed. If you cannot do this, or one of you declares incorrectly, you will all suffer death. You are able to discuss amongst yourselves a plan for achieving this goal, but as already stated, can do nothing to inform any person of the colour of their hat. Finally, there is at least one red hat and at least one blue hat amongst you; that is to say all your hats are not the same colour.

Unfortunately, Merlin was one of the casualties of battle, so the King and your fellow knights are looking to you, Lord of the Hourglass, for salvation.

What plan do you come up with to allow one of the bunch to determine their hat colour and save you all?

Key facts

- Group of men each wearing a hat.

- The hats are either red or blue.
- There is at least one hat of each colour.
- It is forbidden to discuss the colour of your hat in any way.
- If someone can stand up and correctly say the colour of their hat, then all the men will be set free.
- If no one can stand up, or someone stands up and announces their colour incorrectly then all men will be killed.

Challenge

Before everyone is given their hats, you are given time to discuss your options and to formulate a scheme that will enable one of the group to discover their hat colour.

27

In an undeniably silly move, Richard, free and able to leave this accursed country, decides instead to go for one last Mongolian hurrah. 'After all, two fights in the bush are worth seven eggs on the steppes', he reasons.

Unable to dissuade him from this course of action, his advisors however do manage to get Richard to concede that without help they will once again be on the receiving end of a good thrashing. While no immediate allies present themselves, once Richard's men start bandying about purses bulging with gold, 'friends' begin to appear. On the face of it, the warlord, and indeed feuding brother-in-law of Genghis, Eräsk Vanck Bastranktz appears the most promising.

Always keen to get one over on his overbearing brother, Eräsk agrees to provide the services of his clan in return for fiduciary recompense. Only sixty-three members of Genghis's entourage remain with their leader, and Eräsk assures Richard his men will be able to kill them all. When it comes to payment however, things get more complicated. Eräsk demands to be paid using a priceless gold chain he spied amongst Richard's Arabian haul. It had been stolen from the Sultan of Agrabar and, in a cataclysmically contrived coincidence, is a straight chain made up of sixty-three individual links. Richard reluctantly agrees, but due to the exorbitant value of the chain refuses to pay Eräsk up front. Eräsk on the other hand, ever suspicious of Westerners and Bush's foreign policy, refuses to be paid afterwards for fear of Richard reneging on the deal.

 etc.

Figure 2 A section of the priceless gold chain

Luckily, a compromise is reached: After each successful slaying Richard will hand over one link of the chain, thus protecting both parties from a royal stitch-up.

However, there is a minor complication: Eräsk doesn't want the beauty of the chain to be tarnished beyond repair, and therefore demands that no more than three breaks are made in the chain. Richard and his closest advisors are completely stymied, and so you are called in to sort things out.

How do you ensure that Eräsk can receive one link per killing right up to the sixty-third without making more than three breaks in the chain?

Schtümper.

Key facts

- Sixty-three link, straight chain.
- No more than three links must be broken.

Challenge

Suggest a way that Richard can pay one link per killing until all sixty-three are dead, without breaking the chain more than three times.

28

RIVERS OF LAVA AT THE GATES OF HELL

Unfortunately, once again your brilliant solution has been wasted. This time not by Merlin's incompetence as an astronomer, not even by Richard's unfaltering pride, but instead by the fickle, fair-weather friendship offered by the Bastranktz Clan. For, on the day of the battle, Eräsk and his men chose to leave Richard in the lurch and not turn up.

After watching most of his men dispatched by the Mongol hordes, Richard bravely challenged Genghis to a duel to the death, winner takes all. Genghis agreed, and they both got pretty much what they signed up for: death.

Riven from their bodies both Richard and Genghis have been summoned to the gates of heaven. Curiously, Bloody Mary is also there, several hundred years ahead of schedule, but there nonetheless and it's rude to ask questions.

St Peter looks up each of their biographies on his laptop

and, after lots of disappointed head shaking, announces that not one of them is able to enter into heaven. It isn't all doom and gloom though, he explains, as none of them has quite killed enough people to qualify for automatic entry to hell either. (Entry standards were higher in those days.) Therefore they are all to be taken to Purgatory where their souls will be weighed and their fates decided by a cooking balance.

The gates to Purgatory stand on the opposite side of the river to heaven, so therefore they will all have to cross over to the other side. Unfortunately, Peter's small boat will only allow him to transport one passenger over the river at a time. Normally this wouldn't be a cause for concern, but as both Richard and Mary are bloodlusting religious fanatics, Peter can't afford to leave either of them alone with Genghis, as they would most certainly kill him. Again.

How can he transport the three of them safely across to the other side of the river?

NB: It is a river of lava, and falling into it will take you straight to the raging inferno that is hell. And of course there are sharks in the river: Hell sharks.

NB 2: Only Peter knows how to control the boat as it is a holy boat.

Key facts

- Only one person can go in the boat with Peter at a time.

- Richard and/or Mary cannot be left with Genghis unless Peter is there also, for they shalt surely kill him.

Challenge

Get Richard, Mary and Genghis safely to the other side of the river.

PART VI

Good versus Basten

Ever since Gaston returned as Erik's number two in the wake of the plutonium debacle, he has been growing increasingly frustrated with the direction the company is taking. Erik's focus on notoriety over profits is hampering company growth and Gaston has decided that it is time to usurp his mentor, take the helm himself and usher in a new dawn of VBC skulduggery.

Gaston rightly concludes that the best time to depose Erik is when he is relaxing in isolation on his private Mexican island retreat of Mucho Pollo. Although unprotected by henchmen, Gaston knows that Erik has other security measures – a plethora of cunning and fiendish traps, designed by Erik himself and sprinkled about the island. Gaston reasons that the traps would most likely be so villainous that their solution and his subsequent safe passage would be beyond his own mastery of logic.

He thus decides to recruit assistants from history's rich vein of problem-solving genii to neutralise the danger and to clear a path to Erik's master chamber. Using quantum mechanics, necromancy and a spot of magic, he teleports the four greatest logicians of all time to the island: Manchesterano, Jemima, Richard and Merlin.

For respective reasons our problem-solvers are champing at the bit to take up the challenge: Jemima ever keen to rid the world of Erik's size 13 carbon footprint; Manchesterano to exact compensation for his unfair dismissal from VBC Taxidermy; Richard to avenge the dishonourable betrayal of Erik's forefathers; and Merlin for one last shake of the stick at 'The Man'.

So off they go – to the final showdown ...

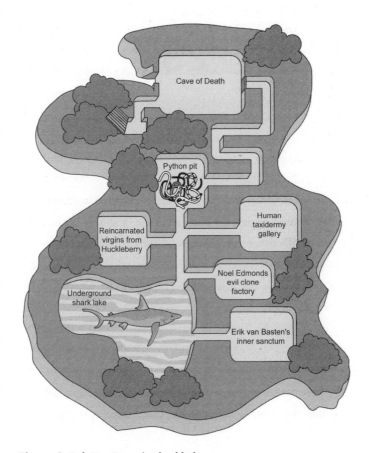

Figure 3 Erik Van Basten's island hideout

29

While Gaston knew nothing of the traps and challenges our familiar foursome are to encounter, he was able to provide the gang with a basic schematic of Erik's lair along with other titbits of Van Basten trivia.

According to the plans, the entrance to Erik's stronghold is concealed beneath dense foliage that covers the entire surface of Mucho Pollo. A trapdoor is located somewhere towards the centre of the island, so the gang set off in that direction. Unfortunately, their movements through the undergrowth have tripped all manner of detection devices and sent the island's first security measure springing into action.

Sensing intruders, the system ignites a strip of foliage running the entire breadth of the island, so that the prevailing wind will blow a wall of fire in the direction of our infiltrating friends.

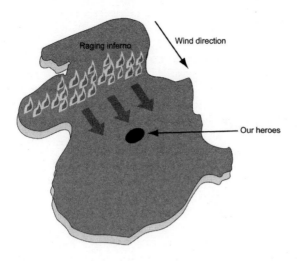

Figure 4 The gang face a fiery end

Where can they run? The entire island is covered in plant growth that, due to the extreme Mexican heat, is as dry as firewood. They can't go into the sea as there are certainly sharks in it, and there are no rivers or lakes in the island they could use to extinguish the fire or shelter within.

They don't quite have the ability to change the direction of the wind but they do have tremendous ingenuity and the few possessions you might normally expect to take on a mission to bring down an evil genius, e.g. tent, kettle, matches, fish tank, etc.

However, with no one around to help, how can they avoid joining the charred remains of the all those tourists who ignored the 'PRIVATE – NO ENTRY' signs?

Key facts

- On an island with no escape.
- Raging fire blowing in your direction.

Challenge

Avoid death.

30

Managing to avoid roasting for thirty minutes at gas mark 7, our friends locate the retreat's hidden entrance and drop down into the caverns beneath the island. In the darkness, they soon stumble upon the next of Erik's traps: a locked door with a rather devious locking mechanism.

Hanging aside the door are eight identical keys and the following message:

Dearest Intruder. You have somehow made it past my raging fire trap so you are surely brave, but are you cunning? We shall soon see.

You will notice eight keys hanging adjacent to this notice. Seven of them are identical decoys and if placed within the lock to the cell will, unfortunately, result in death, death and more death, as all respiratory privileges will be rescinded. The last of the keys will open the door. The only difference between this eighth key and the others is that it is marginally heavier.

In order to discover which of the keys is not a deadly decoy I have generously provided you with an old-fashioned weighing balance which will only work twice.

If you attempt to use the balance more than twice, or insert an incorrect key into the lock, the area will be hermetically sealed and you'll suffer a slow, suffocating death.

How can you discover which of the eight keys is the heaviest and therefore the only one that will open the door and allow you to continue your mission?

Key facts

- Seven identical dummy keys.
- An eighth key, the correct one, identical in all but weight: marginally heavier than the others.
- You have an old-fashioned weighing balance – you know, one with a pan on each side.
- You are allowed only two weighings.

Challenge

Identify the correct key and proceed into the Van Basten Lair.

31

Opening the door they pass into a long corridor heading deep into the bowels of the Van Basten bastion. By this point Erik's security measures are becoming more lethal, for as they close the door behind them, the corridor starts to fill up with poisonous Dijon mustard gas. Luckily, their insider knowledge alerted them to Erik's proclivity for the substance, so they came prepared for such an attack.

In order to counteract the effects of the mustard gas the gang brought along two types of pills, Killabasten and Sharkenkampf. When taken together in equal dose they neutralise the effect of the gas, but if taken in an unmatched dose the pills are fatal and may even cause death.

As the corridor is slowly filling up with the gas, the team pass out the pills, each taking the prescribed dose. However, when the pill jars are passed to Richard he manages to mess the whole thing up by accidentally tipping two Killabasten pills into his hand along with one Sharkenkampf pill. Normally this wouldn't be a problem, but, in the zenith of unlikelihood, the German pharmaceuticals company that manufactures the pills has made the two types appear identical: they are the same size, colour, IQ, weight, smell and, as such, are completely indistinguishable.

What can they do? They can't afford to waste the pills and start again as they don't know what evil lurks behind the next corner. Furthermore, misdosing would be the most costly of mistakes, and Richard certainly doesn't want to die. Again.

So what must they do? How can they ensure they give him the correct dose without wasting any of these precious pills?

Key facts

- There are two types of pill that are indistinguishable from each other.
- One of each pill is needed to neutralise the deadly gas.
- Richard messes up and tips an extra Killabasten pill into his hand, so now he has three pills.

Challenge

Make sure Richard takes the correct dose of one pill each without wasting any pills.

32

Surviving the gas chamber malarkey, Manny, Richard, Merlin and Jemima straddle the snake pit, overcome Erik's horde of reincarnated Huckleberry virgins and arrive at the underground lake. On the far shore, the Van Basten inner sanctum is at last in sight.

Discovering Erik's fishing boat, they jump in and begin to row across the lake to impending victory. However, the security system is not yet ready to concede defeat and activates what is probably the second most expensive trap Erik has ever created.

All of a sudden the foursome hear a grinding from above and the whole roof of the cavern starts slowly, yet inexorably to lower. Furthermore, all exits from the lake are blocked by blast doors that rise out of the cave floor. This all leaves our heroes trapped between the lowering roof above, the shark infested waters below and the blast doors around. Sharkendeath ist imminent.

Whipping out the plans of the hideaway, Jemima searches for an answer to their calamitous situation. Fortunately there is mention of the trap, but she is hardly encouraged by what she reads: the only way to cause the system to retract is to somehow raise the water level of the entire lake!

Scouring the cavern, the team notice that all around there are tiny sensors located marginally above the current water level. This, combined with the inspected blueprints leads them to deduce correctly that in order to activate the retraction of the roof and blast doors, the sensors must all register an increase in water level at the same time. This unfortunately rules out making waves in order to trick a particular sensor into thinking the level has increased. Or throwing fish at it. No. No. No.

All that's in the boat with our protagonists are some fish from Erik's early morning catch and their boundless cunning.

How the Darwin can they raise the water level, retract the roof and continue on with their quest?

Izzzittt.

Key facts

- Stuck in a boat on a lake.
- Only possessions in boat are some dead fish.
- And, yes, there are sharks in the lake.

Challenge

Increase the water level of the lake.

PART VII

The end of all things

At last they arrive at their final destination – the sanctuary of the evil genius. At this inner level, this nerve centre of the Van Basten stronghold, the defences are surprisingly light. Erik had not countenanced the possibility of intruders surviving such a succession of heinous traps. Recumbent within his private chamber, he is six hours into an Ally McBeal all-nighter when his door is kicked open and Manchesterano and friends storm into the room.

'What devils are these that have breached my fortress? What creatures could possibly have overcome my genius? They cannot be real – I must be dreaming. It is … not … conceivable …'

Alas for Erik it isn't a dream and his face soon becomes

ashen – for Gaston has followed the team through the traps and chooses now to make his triumphant entrance.

'Et tu Gaston? Has it really come to this? Invading my summer retreat, ruining my McBeal marathon and trying to take over my empire? Confound you Gaston!

Well, you may have won the battle. In fact, you may even have won the war, but by Merlin's sleeve you'll never take me alive.' A trap door opens beneath him and with a puff of smoke, a burst of flame and a final flash of genius he disappears into a fiery pit below.

Our jubilant party return to civilisation, feeling quite chuffed with having reduced the evil quotient in the universe by one. Gaston promises to run VBC with greener intentions. He rewards our team members with one hundred gold coins and enough M&Ms to choke a bison. All appears to be well in the world …

However …

33

A few months on from the Mucho Pollo mission, Gaston and the gang began to suspect that something was deeply wrong. They had all started to experience nausea, vomiting and vivid hallucinations of Erik himself. They realised Erik's farewell trick was not limited to his miraculous disappearance.

With a battle-weary Richard dying (again) three months after leaving the island, our protagonists realised the magnitude of the problem. Somehow, in a masterpiece of posthumous cunning, Erik had managed to infect his would-be captors with a deadly mutant variant of swine flu.

What's more, shortly after Richard's departure, members of the general population began dying having registered Erik hallucinations as a symptom during their demise. Our team's worst fears were realised. They had all become unwitting agents of Erik's contamination plan and his evil virus was now at large.

Fearful of a full blown pandemic, the governments of the world were quick to act. In a show of international cooperation not seen since the West faked the moon, G8 opted for a rapidly implemented containment approach: anyone claiming to see the haunting face of Erik would have their passport rescinded and be exiled to Wales to await the onset of the full force of the virus.

In the first few months following the enactment of the G8 decree, the exiled population of Wales increased to dramatic levels. More recently, however, the numbers of those coming forward complaining of the virus's symptoms has almost completely stopped, resulting in the G8 claiming their containment protocols a runaway success.

However, Gaston, Manny, Jemima and Merlin were less disposed towards celebration. Firstly, they were all infected with the virus and could die at any time. Secondly, as first hand recipients of Erik's past exploits, they were highly doubtful that his life's concluding act of cunning would be so easily countered. Their fears were confirmed when Gaston conducted a survey throughout the VBC global employee network. The results were overwhelmingly bad – over 25% of the staff were suffering from the Van Basten hallucinations, yet were not coming forward for fear of having to spend the final months of their lives in the Millennium Stadium.

Showing his evidence of widespread infection to G8 in an attempt to make them reassess their containment programme,

Gaston was firmly rebuked – after all, he was number to the fiend who started the whole thing. The G8 did however concede that if it could be proved that the global infection rate was much higher than they believed then they would invest the trillions of dollars required for developing the cure. However, highly suspicious of both Gaston's criminal pedigree and the capitalist morals of the drugs companies who stood to make a killing, G8 would not accept a secret ballot, or anything that didn't provide a name alongside each entry/answer in a survey. Furthermore, each person surveyed would have to be able to confirm the answer they had provided to prevent all manner of double and fake entries.

The problem is that no individual wants to own up to having the virus because they would then be quarantined. At the same time, however, everyone with the virus understands the crucial importance of being counted in the survey in order to ensure the funds are made available to find the cure.

And so we find our friends in a quandary. Somewhat disconsolate and feeling guilty at having spread this global pandemic, they have committed themselves to completing the survey and to proving to the governments that they must invest in finding a cure. However, they are pretty much stumped.

How can they survey the population, making sure that anyone who has the virus admits to it, in such a way that this knowledge could never be used against them directly?

It is time for you to prove your worth and help Manchesterano, Jemima, Merlin and Gaston save the world and ensure that Erik's final act does not bring an end to humanity. What's more, there's a reward in it for you. Get it right and you could win £1000 and find yourself meeting Manny and friends in the sequel! For details, see the competition page at the back of this book.

Key facts

- People know they have the virus.
- People want to tell the truth.
- The infected need there to be no way of tying their answer to whether or not they have the virus. It is not enough to have the knowledge in code or locked away securely – there must be no information in an individual's answer.
- Your survey results must be able to demonstrate the extent of the spread throughout the population.

Challenge

Design the 'impossible' survey and you could take home £1000!

Trains of thought to avoid

Looking elsewhere for further information on the Van Basten virus. Firstly, everything you need to solve the problem is in the question itself, and secondly, there is no such virus. We hope.

Anything to do with sharks – Nein sharken ist answer-gladbach.

 to the power of sellotape

Problem 1

In order to get twenty-seven individual pieces you must separate all mini-cubes from every piece they are touching.

Problem 2

Forget about drawing it all out on a chart from the first round. Working out byes etc. will take far too long. Start thinking about it from the other end.

Problem 3

After thirty days everyone was infected. Work backwards.

Problem 4

How much was actually paid in total? Not given to the waiter, but actually paid?

Problem 5

The key is the fact that the bullets are adjacent. In consecutive chambers. Next to each other.

Problem 6

She's 99% fat to start with. Therefore she's 1% bone, muscle, etc. When she loses weight where will it come from?

Problem 7

Possibly the finest problem in the book and a version of a problem that has had more written about it in error than possibly any other logic problem of all time.

What's the chance of getting the Osama door with the audience's first pick?

Problem 8

Try opening the batches of pills.

Problem 9

You have an infinite supply of packets but will you get an infinite number of different readings?

Problem 10

Think of the simplest possible case. Reduce the problem so

people can pick from a much narrower range, e.g. between £0 and £10 – even £0 and £1.

Then try it with just two people.

Problem 11

Reduce the problem to a simpler case. Instead of amounts from one to forty, what about one to ten or maybe even one to five?

Problem 12

Reduce to the simplest possible case. What if there were only one of each colour? If that doesn't help, increase complexity gradually, e.g. two M&Ms of each colour etc. Remember there are two steps to this problem. The first is selecting the jar, the second is pulling out an M&M from the jar you select.

Problem 13

This is another of the recursive logic problems. Work backwards from the simplest possible, non-trivial case, i.e. imagine there were just two people.

Problem 14

Think about what is random in the situation and what isn't.

Problem 15

Reduce to a simpler case. One bottle is obviously ridiculous but what about maybe ten bottles, one of which is poisoned?

Problem 16

Reduce to a very simple case. Try it with ten toilets only and see if you can work out any patterns.

Problem 17

Manchesterano's revelation brings no new information to the table, but the fact that he announces with certainty that there is at least one mobile phone user starts a chain of events …

Problem 18

Since the byguin cannot outrun Manny's boat while on dry land, it has to think of a strategy that will not involve making a direct dash for it. Therefore anything involving straight line motion will not work.

Problem 19

This is a very clever problem that definitely involves the art of being counter-intuitive. Think of all the most logical things that Gaston and Jemima could do and then set about doing the opposite – the last thing you would expect. It actually requires them to go back before they can go forward.

Problem 20

What would happen if you switched all the lights on? Would that tell you anything about which switch controlled which light?

Problem 21

Work backwards. You need to end up with 6 litres in the 8 litre container and 6 litres in the 12 litre container. (You couldn't fit 6 litres into the 5 litre one!)

Problem 22

How long does it take for any pair crossing the bridge?

Problem 23

There is no virtue in considering cutting the fuses in any way. Since they are irregular, you would have no way of knowing how long it would take to burn a certain segment of either fuse. The only thing you are certain of is the fact that it takes sixty seconds to burn through either one.

Problem 24

Think about an hourglass. It is a bit like a container with no markings, only useful if it runs its entire course. There's no way of knowing when half the time has passed, only when all the time has gone.

Problem 25

Once you have worked out the relative speed of approach you can work out the time it takes for the armies to reach each other.

Problem 26

Reduce it to the simplest possible case, i.e. two people. Remember there is at least one red and one blue hat. This may appear too trivial a solution but it is good practice for what is coming.

Problem 27

Think about what happens when you break a link in the chain. How many pieces do you get?

Problem 28

This is actually a re-formulation of a classic thinking problem involving boats and goats and chickens and foxes, and stuff like that. And corn.

Problem 29

There is no possible escape from the island so it is more about finding ways to remain on the island yet not become burnt to death.

Problem 30

You can only get any sensible information out of a pan balance if you weigh equal numbers of keys against each other but you don't have to use all the keys in a weighing.

Problem 31

Think counter-intuitively. You already have too many pills. Intuition dictates you should try to put one back.

Problem 32

One of the ways the lake's level could be raised is by adding more water but you only have what is actually in your boat. Another way to raise the lake's level is to put something into the lake that wasn't in it before which will displace water and therefore raise the water level of the whole lake.

Problem 1

Think of the faces of the centre piece.

Problem 2

With 4,619 teams producing only one winner, how many losers were there?

Problem 3

The infection rate doubled every day, so if you're working backwards it halved every day.

Problem 4

How much did the meal cost? How much did the waiter pocket?

Problem 5

If there are two chambers with bullets next to each other, then there are four empty chambers next to each other.

Problem 6

If she weighed 300 kg when 99% fat, how much did the other 1% weigh?

Problem 7

Does it make any difference that the host knows what's behind each door?

Problem 8

If you weighed ten pills from random batches could you tell how many of them were contaminated?

Problem 9

Since the packaging material is identical in mass, the only difference in readings between packs is due to the different numbers of M&Ms inside the packs.

Problem 10

Since you are not choosing simply the average of all other choices, rather you are choosing this average divided by three, what will happen if everyone thinks logically and anticipates what the others do?

Problem II

Try working through all the amounts from 1 g upwards. Obviously you need a 1 g mass to do 1 g. And you need another 1 g mass to do 2 g etc., but you could have a 2 g mass and then you'd be able to do up to 3 g with 2 masses, etc.

Problem I2

Go with two sweets of each colour. You have limited possibilities. Try to see which will give you the best chance of getting the red M&M.

Problem I3

Expand the problem step by step and see what logical conclusions you come to. Remember that everyone in this problem is a perfectly logical being, not a human.

Problem I4

Imagine turning up at Heathrow with the idea of catching the first plane to any of the destinations. What's the first thing you would do when you got there?

Problem 15

You can approach this from two directions:

1. Manchesterano's staff members' perspective: testers can drink from more than one bottle.
2. Bottle perspective: bottles can be sampled by more than one tester.

Problem 16

The number of times a toilet ends up getting toggled depends on how many smaller numbers multiply into it. These are called factors. In the case of toilet 40, the numbers 1, 2, 4, 5, 8, 10, 20, 40 all multiply into 40 and so are all factors of 40. These always come in pairs since they multiply together to equal 40, e.g. 10×4, 8×5 etc.

Problem 17

Reduce to the simplest possible case: one wife and one husband.

Problem 18

When you swing a long pole in a circle, your hand moves much more slowly than the far end of the pole. The circle that the end of the pole follows has a much greater circumference than the circle in which your hand moves.

Problem 19

Instead of decrypting an encrypted message, what else could Jemima do with it?

Problem 20

What if you switched one or two of them on? How could you get the most information out of the system?

Problem 21

With no markings on containers you can only perform two operations exactly:

1. empty a container completely; or
2. fill a container completely.

Problem 22

Is it necessary for the fastest person to bring the torch back each time?

Problem 23

Since you need a time that is less than either fuse's burn time, how can you increase the speed at which they burn (not through using an accelerant or anything like that — just through the use of cunning).

Problem 24

You have an eight-hour and a five-hour hourglass. What is crucial about these numbers in relation to the desired total of eleven hours?

Problem 25

Can you work out how fast the armies are approaching each other?

Problem 26

Extend the problem to the next least complex scenario, i.e. three people. If you are one of the three people, there are only two possible hat combinations in front of you. How would you react to each one?

Problem 27

Each time you break a link you get that link as a single piece and two other pieces.

Problem 28

The trick is in realising you have limited options – you have to play around with it.

Problem 29

What does a fire need in order to continue burning?

Problem 30

There are actually three possible results when you weigh equal numbers of keys:

1. The balance tips to one side.
2. The balance tips to the other side.
3. The balance is level.

Problem 31

Can you reduce the imbalance towards Killabasten? There are twice as many Killabasten pills as Sharkenkampf pills.

Problem 32

A third way to raise the water level is to remove something from the lake that was denser than water and to put it into the boat.

Problem 1

Can you separate the centre piece from all the pieces its faces are touching in fewer than six cuts?

Problem 2

In a simple knockout tournament, how many matches are needed to eliminate a team?

Problem 3

So from everybody infected to half the population infected took how many days going backwards?

Problem 4

This problem is illusory, it's the closest thing in the book to misdirection.

Problem 5

If an empty chamber has been just fired, what are the chances that the following chamber is also empty? Compare the without spinning again position with the re-spin option.

Problem 6

Since the actual mass of the bone etc. remains the same but the mass of fat decreases due to the diet, the percentage of non-fat increases as the percentage of fat decreases.

Problem 7

What if there were one hundred doors and the host knows what's behind each door and he opens ninety-eight of them? Should you switch then? Does it make any difference how many doors there are?

Problem 8

What would happen if you weighed ten pills from each batch?

Problem 9

Imagine you have two readings – 342 g and 327 g – the difference in mass between these two packs is equal to a multiple of the mass of a single M&M, since it results from the difference of a whole number of M&Ms between the two packs.

Problem 10

The mean of all amounts from £0 to £100 is £50, and so they should choose x (the mean divided by 3) as £50/3 = £17. However, if everyone thinks logically like this and they all choose £17, the mean will now be £17.

This means that x = £17/3 = £6 (to nearest whole number) and so on.

Where does it end?

Problem 11

The type of balance where you have two pans either side that balance off against each other allows you to put masses on both sides. The initial strategy is to put the masses on the opposite side of the item you are weighing. But you can also put masses on the same side as the object being weighed. This reduces the number of weights required.

Problem 12

Can you organise it so that if you choose the right jar you will certainly get a red?

Problem 13

Remember at least half the people must vote for any idea. Not more than half, at least half. Big difference.

Problem 14

OK, so you've turned up and you've seen the departures board to the three locations. Even though there are the same number of flights to each city, what determines which one you actually catch?

Problem 15

Think now of making sure that every tester has drunk from one particular arrangement. In the case of only a few bottles, you could certainly work out which bottle was poisoned if no two testers had drunk from exactly the same selection of bottles.

Example
Tester one drinks from bottles one, two and four.
Tester two from bottles two and three and five.
Tester three from bottles four, five and six.
If tester one died – it was bottle one.
If tester two and three died – it was bottle five.
If tester three died – it was bottle six.
If tester one and three died – it was bottle four.

Problem 16

The key thing is to work out whether a toilet ends up on or off. Toilets that get toggled an even number of times will end up turned off and those that get toggled an odd number of times will end up turned on. However, if factors always come in pairs because they multiply together, how can a number have an odd number of factors?

Problem 17

Gradually increase complexity. What would happen if there were two couples? Then three?

Problem 18

Manny will always try to get to the point on the edge of the floe that he thinks the byguin is heading for. If the byguin doesn't head towards the edge but instead follows a circle fairly close to the centre, what will happen?

Problem 19

Since you can never send encryption keys, the only person who can ever take off a key is the sender of the message.

Problem 20

Does a lamp give off anything other the light?

Problem 21

Working backwards: to get 6 litres in an 8 litre container, you can either put in 6 litres from other sources or you can empty out 2 litres from a full 8 litre container.

Problem 22

Which guy or guys do you definitely *not* want to make more than one journey?

Problem 23

What would happen if you were to light a fuse at both ends?

Problem 24

If you know how much sand/time has passed through an hourglass at any point, you can flip it over to measure that length of time again.

Problem 25

Merlin keeps moving backwards and forwards until the armies meet, so his journey time is the same as the armies'.

Problem 26

Sticking with the three person scenario. If you don't react, what does that tell the other people?

Problem 27

You are going to end up with three single links from the three breaks (Second hint). That'll take care of the first three kills. What do you do for the fourth kill?

Problem 28

There's nothing to stop St Peter taking someone back across the river to heaven if necessary.

Problem 29

My grandfather always used to say 'fight fire with fire', which is probably why he was kicked out of the fire brigade. Seriously, this problem is perhaps one of the most counter-intuitive of all the problems in the book.

Problem 30

You don't actually have to weigh the heavier key to identify it. If the balance is level, it tells you that the correct key is in the group that you didn't weigh.

Problem 3I

As long as the correct dosage is taken, both pills can be taken at the same time.

Problem 32

Consider a floating boat. In order for the boat to be supported by the water (i.e. float), it needs to displace an amount of water equal to its weight. A very heavy cargo such as gold bars will cause a boat to displace a lot of water.

However if the gold bars are in the lake and have of course sunk to the bottom of the lake, they will only be displacing an amount of water equal to their volume.

Problem 1

Oh come on!

Problem 2

So how many matches do you need to generate 4,618 losing teams?

Problem 3

And how many days until only 25% were infected?

Problem 4

Actually it is blatant misdirection. Look carefully at what's happened.

Problem 5

If Erik spins again, the probability that he will select an empty chamber is 4/6 or 66.67%. If he does not spin again, the chamber following an empty chamber will be his. Of the four empty chambers, how many are followed by a bullet?

Problem 6

At 98% fat her non-fat component has doubled in percentage terms although its mass is still 1% of 300 kg, i.e. 3 kg.

Problem 7

Reverse the problem. If the audience decides to switch, what's the probability they don't get Osama?

Problem 8

What would happen if you weighed different numbers of pills from each batch?

Problem 9

Patterns in the differences between packs will become apparent after a large enough number of weighings.

Problem 10

Remember that these are all perfectly logical geniuses, not human beings who would no doubt not be able to follow this pattern through to its logical conclusion.

Problem 11

Now see how far you can go covering all possible amounts from 1 g upwards. There are actually four weights. The first two are 1 g and 3 g weights.

Problem 12

Can you organise it so that even if you don't pick the jar that is certainly red you still have a good chance of getting a red?

Problem 13

A feature of a perfectly logical being is that he/she will always choose a strategy that will maximise personal gain, even if it is not even remotely 'fair' in the common usage of the word.

Problem 14

Do the flights leave at the same times each day? Or do they change all the time? Reduce the problem to one flight per day per destination.

Problem 15

Can you extend this idea by thinking of the bottles as an array from 1 to 2,000, each particular bottle having a unique combination of testers that sampled it?

Problem 16

Look at your results for your simple case of only ten toilets. The toilet numbers that ended up electrified were toggled an odd number of times so they must have had an odd number of factors. What type of numbers are these, and how many of them are there between 1 and 100 inclusive?

Problem 17

You could try working backwards. Consider the case where you are one of the wives. You know there are seventy-nine errant husbands and you therefore expect all seventy-nine wives only know of only seventy-eight mobile phone users, since they don't know about their own and so on. You expect them to think that there will be carnage on the seventy-eighth day. I've said too much …

Problem 18

Using some sort of circular motion, can the byguin ensure that Manny has to travel more than four times the distance that it does?

Problem 19

What if Jemima put a further encryption on the message before sending it back to Gaston?

Problem 20

With three lights and only two states, ON or OFF, it is quite impossible to solve. However there is another state: A lamp that is now OFF could have either never been ON, or, ON first and then switched OFF.

Problem 21

In order to pour out exactly 2 litres from the 8 litre container, you need a '2 litre space' in another container e.g. 3 litres already in the 5 litre container.
See where I'm going with this?

Problem 22

The technique of modelling works really well with this one. So try working it through with action figures/fruit/small children.

Problem 23

Not all ends have to be lit at the same time.

Problem 24

Try starting both hourglasses at the same time and see where you get.

Problem 25

If you know his journey time and his speed you should be able to work out how far he's gone! (Speed = Distance/Time or something.)

Problem 26

Think of a routine to go through that would be related to time, such as if there are five red hats. These five people stand up on the fifth minute.

Problem 27

There's nothing to stop Eräsk giving you one link back in exchange for two more.

Problem 28

Draw it out or play it out with Star Wars figures.

Problem 29

What are the three things that fire needs to survive? How can you take one of them away by using fire itself?

Problem 30

Try dividing the keys into two equal groups and one unequal group. What results are possible when you weigh the two equal groups? Can you repeat the strategy once you have narrowed down the number of keys?

Problem 31

Mix and match. You have no restrictions on how the pills can be physically manipulated.

Problem 32

What can you think of that is denser than water that can be easily reached and placed into the boat or indeed lured into the boat by means of bait?

Problem 1

Since the centre piece is joined at each face to other pieces, i.e. surrounded by six other cubes, no matter how many times you rearrange other pieces after each cut, you need at least six cuts to isolate the centre piece. Therefore six cuts is the minimum.

Problem 2

Since there were 4,619 teams in the competition, there must have been one winner and 4,618 losers. In a simple knockout tournament a team is eliminated when it loses a match. Therefore you need 4,618 matches to produce 4,618 losers.

Problem 3

Since everyone was infected after thirty days and the infection rate was doubling every day, the day before everyone was infected, 50% were infected and two days before, 25%. Therefore two days before thirty days only 25% were infected. So twenty-eight days is the answer.

Problem 4

There is no missing pound! This is an example of blatant misdirection. It is pretty clever though because the amounts are quite close and it shows you how people can be easily confused with very basic maths. What you have to remember is that the diners parted with some money that paid for both the meal and for the waiter's tip.

Looking at the numbers:

They each paid £9 giving a total paid of £27. The meal cost £25. The difference, i.e. £2, was pocketed by the waiter as a tip. If you then add on the £1 change each person received you're left with £25 + £2 + (3 × £1) = £30.

Problem 5

The six chambers of the barrel are in the following sequence: (E = empty, F = full) E – E – E – E – F – F.

An empty chamber has just been fired by Mel C, i.e. one of the four 'E' slots. Only one of these is followed by an 'F' so there is only a 1/4 chance that Erik will get a bullet. This means that there is a 3/4 or 75% chance of surviving without re-spinning.

This is better than the 66% chance of surviving should he spin again, and therefore it is better to shoot without doing anything to the barrel. Of course, taking the bullets out, replacing them in a random way and spinning still only gives him a 66% chance of survival.

Problem 6

The quantity that is conserved is the non-fat matter. This is 1% of 300 kg i.e. 3 kg. You don't have to worry about the fat loss, you just know that at the end of the diet her non-fat is now 2% of her final mass. However it must still be equal to 3 kg since it is unchanged. If 3 kg is 2% of her total mass, then 1% is 1.5 kg, 10% is 15 kg and 100% is 150 kg.

So her mass has dropped from the astonishing 300 kg to the only mildly less absurd 150 kg, but since she has lost half her mass understandably the doctor was chuffed.

Problem 7

The astonishing answer is that the audience doubles its chances of getting Osama if they switch doors. Their chances go from 1/3 if they stick to 2/3 if they switch. Let me explain.

Since there is only one Osama and three doors, there is a 1/3 chance of getting Osama with the first pick. Undisputed.

There are two options for the audience: to switch or to stick with their original pick.

Let's assume they decide to switch.

In a switching strategy they can only *not* get Osama if they chose him with their first pick. Since there is a 1/3 chance of getting Osama with their first pick, there is therefore a 1/3 chance that they will lose or a 2/3 chance they will win.

Most of the general public and many mathematicians fail to get the correct answer when first presented with this problem. The reason many people get it wrong is because they assume that the opening of the door that brings forth George Bush is actually a random event, therefore there can be no information in it. However it is not random since the host knows what is behind the doors, and so he can always produce either George Bush or Kermit since the audience cannot with their first pick select both of these options.

A common mistake is to think that since there are now two doors and two choices, the chance of selecting either one of them has gone up to 50:50. This is incorrect. If you stick with your original pick, there can be no difference in probability at any point in the game. You made the choice when there was a 1/3 chance, therefore it must always be a 1/3 chance since the host knows what is behind the doors.

If there were 100 doors, as long as the host knows where Osama is, he can open 98 doors, leaving just the one you picked and the one that Osama is behind. Would you still decide to stick with your original choice with a 1/100 probability, or would you change when there are only two doors left?

Of course if the host had no information about the doors and opened 98 doors at random and Osama had still not shown, then you would be correct in thinking that a changing strategy would now give you a 1/2 chance of getting Osama.

Another way of looking at it is this:

The sticking strategy has a 1/3 chance of giving you Osama.

Since there are only two outcomes, Osama or not, the probability through switching plus the probability through sticking must be equal to one. (Osama *must* be behind one of the two remaining doors.)

(Probability of getting Osama through sticking) + (Probability of getting Osama through switching) = 1

Since sticking = 1/3, switching must be = 2/3

Of course, people will always disagree with this answer, despite the brilliant explanation, so I invite anyone who is unsatisfied to run it as an experiment. Thirty tries for each strategy should be ample to calculate the probabilities.

Problem 8

You take different numbers of pills from each batch: one from the first, two from the second, three from the third … and so on until you finally take ten from the tenth batch. Then you weigh this collection of pills. The key then will be how much lower the reading is than what you would have got had you been weighing 'pure' pills only.

Let's imagine that the difference between the reading you expected and the reading you got was 5 mg. Each contaminated pill is 1 mg less than a normal pill, so if the total of all pills is 5 mg less than expected, that means you must have five contaminated pills in your sample.

So if you took one pill from batch one, two pills from

batch two etc., then five dodgy pills would mean that batch five was the faulty batch.

For completeness:

The expected reading in this strategy is (9 mg × however may pills you pulled out).

How many pills would you have pulled out?

$1 + 2 + 3 + 4 + 5 + 6 + 7 + 8 + 9 + 10 = 55$ pills total

Expected reading would have therefore been 9 mg × 55 = 495 mg and the following results would tell you which batch was the stinker:

494 mg = 1 mg less = 1 pill = batch one

493 mg = 2 mg less = 2 pills = batch two

and so on until ...

485 mg = 10 mg less = 10 pills = batch ten

Problem 9

You record the mass of all packs. The smallest difference in mass between any two readings equates to the smallest difference possible in the number of M&Ms i.e. one – a single sweet. Therefore the smallest difference between two weighings would be equal to the mass of an M&M. This only works when dealing with a large enough sample so that you can be fairly sure that you'll have packs with consecutive whole number totals.

Problem 10

This is a recursive logic problem and the only logical amount to choose is £0.

Let's work through it like this:

If people choose between £0 and £100 at random then we would expect the average to be close to £50. Since we are interested in the average divided by three, £50 divided by three would be £16.67. So, the perfectly logical being will choose £17 (being the nearest integer).

However this would then change the average itself, which would now be close to £17. This in turn changes the answer which would then be £17 divided by three or about £6.

Continuing with this train of thought indicates that the only sensible answer to choose is £0. Since everyone is perfectly logical, they know that everyone will choose £0, which means that the prize will be shared equally amongst all contestants.

Problem II

The answer is four measuring weights in the following denominations (all in g): 1, 3, 9 and 27.

Here's how it works:

To balance a dynamite stick weighing 1 g you need a 1 g weight. To balance a 2 g stick you need a 3 g weight on the opposite side of the balance *and* a 1 g weight on the *same* side of the balance.

To balance a 3 g dynamite stick is straightforward, to balance a 4 g dynamite stick you put both 3 g and 1 g weights on the opposite side of the balance. To balance a 5 g dynamite stick you need a new weight equal to 9 g. Since you have a 3 g and a 1 g weight, your total is 4 g. With a new 9 g weight you

can put 4 g on the *same* side of the balance, which is then sub-
tracted from 9 g to give 5 g.

Here's how it works in a table:

A (Dynamite stick)	B (Masses on opposite side)	C (Masses on same side)
1	1	
2	3	1
3	3	
4	3, 1	
5	9	3, 1
6	9	3
7	9, 1	3
8	9	1
9	9	
10	9, 1	
11	9, 3	1
12	9, 3	
13	9, 3, 1	
14	27	9, 3, 1
15	27	9, 3
16	27, 1	9, 3
17	27	9, 1
18	27	9
19	27, 1	9
20	27, 3	9, 1
21	27, 3	9
22	27, 3, 1	9
23	27	3, 1
24	27	3
25	27, 1	3
etc.	all the way	to
40	27, 9, 3, 1	

The dynamite stick (column A) must be exactly equal to the total of the weights on the opposite side of the balance (column B) minus anything that is on the same side as the stick (column C).

The formula can be mathematically reduced to $A = B - C$.

Problem 12

You can organise the sweets to have approximately a 75% chance of getting a red one.

You place one red M&M in the one jar (Jar 1) and all five blue M&Ms and the remaining four red ones in the other. (Jar 2).

The following possibilities arise when you make your choices:

50% chance you pick Jar 1 – leads to 1/1 chance of red.
The probability of picking a red M&M from Jar 1 is 50%.
50% chance you pick Jar 2 – leads to 4/9 chance of red.
The probability of picking a red M&M from Jar 2 is 22%.
Adding up gives an overall chance of red of approximately 72%

Pretty bon, n'est-ce pas?

Problem 13

This is a variation of one of the most famous recursive logic problems of all time. We chose to give it a different setting from the usual one so that people wouldn't just be able to find the answers on the internet. That would deprive you of the pleasure of working things out. Believe me, there is no greater legal pleasure.

Your best proposal is astonishingly 998, 0, 1, 0, 1 for the recipients in order of their ranking:

You – £998

Hairy Back Gary – £0

Third highest ranking apprentice – £1

Fourth apprentice – £0

Lowest ranked apprentice – £1

The reason is that the apprentices are all perfectly logical beings and have no interest in the concept of 'fairness' enshrined in human social behaviour.

The apprentices will vote for a proposal only if it increases their gain.

Let's look at the situation from the simplest possible case. Only the last two apprentices remain. The higher ranked of the two only needs his own vote since one is at least half of two and so he will propose a 1,000:0 split with the lowest ranked apprentice getting nothing.

Therefore the lowest ranked apprentice will vote for any scenario that will prevent it from going down to the last two, as long as it promises more than zero of course.

The next simplest case is when there are only three people left. The highest ranked of the three knows that if his proposal is turned down and the situation goes down to just two apprentices, then the last guy will get nothing. So he knows that the minimum needed to secure the lowest ranking apprentice's vote is £1. So the third highest ranking apprentice would propose a split of £999 – £0 – £1 with the next highest ranking apprentice in the middle getting nothing.

Going back a stage further and Hairy Back Gary, as second highest ranked apprentice, knows that he can win the fourth highest ranked's vote quite easily since that guy will get nothing if it gets down to only three people left. So in a similar way, Gary proposes a £999, £0, £1, £0 split, with the third highest and the lowest ranked apprentices both getting nothing.

So it comes to the five player situation. You know that if your proposal is voted down, as the highest ranked you will die, and Gary will propose the above split. Since all you need to do is secure two other votes, you simply make sure that both of the apprentices who would end up getting nothing if you are killed, get more than nothing from your proposal:

You – highest ranked apprentice – £998

Hairy Back Gary – second highest ranked – £0

Third highest ranking apprentice – £1

Fourth apprentice – 0

Lowest ranked apprentice – £1

Even though it may seem quite disproportionate, both number three and number five will get nothing if they don't accept and £1 is better than nothing.

Of course these are the minimum amounts with perfectly logical beings. Any proposal will be accepted by number three and number five as long as it exceeds the minimum one.

You could propose a £200 split to everyone and this would actually get passed, since the third highest ranked and the lowest ranked will always vote for it.

These results would only work with perfectly logical beings. Humans are much more likely to try to prevent themselves being screwed over by someone even if it means they lose everything. There is a human tendency to choose lose-lose rather than lose-win.

There are several games that indicate this where you have a proposer and an acceptor. A famous one consists of £10 to be shared out between the two of them. The proposer suggests a split, which can either be accepted in which case the money gets shared out as proposed or rejected in which case no money gets shared out at all.

It would make logical sense for the proposer to suggest a 9:1 split since one is better than nothing for the acceptor but human psychology doesn't follow logic: often the acceptor would rather have nothing than have the proposer get nine times what they get!

I'm always reminded of the guy who was ordered to sell his Ferrari and give his wife 50% of the proceeds as part of a divorce settlement. He allegedly sold it for a dollar.

Problem 14

The big realisation is that even though the arrival of Manny's entourage at the terminal is random, the times of the flights are fixed. It is the flight times relative to each other that is important.

Imagine there is only one flight per day per destination. If they were equally spaced, then the chances of getting any particular one of them would be identical. There would be no preference, and you would find equal numbers of specialists in all three locations.

However this is not the case. Imagine what would happen if the Vegas flight was at 10:00, the San Diego flight at 11:36 and the Los Angeles flight at 14:00. If you turned up anytime between 14:00 one day and 10:00 the following day the first flight that came up would be the Vegas flight. You would only catch the San Diego flight if you arrived between 10:00 and 11:36 and you would only catch the Los Angeles flight if you arrived between 11:36 and 14:00.

This means that for random arrivals at Heathrow, Manchesterano's staff would have a 20/24 chance of catching the Vegas flight, a 1.6/24 chance of getting the San Diego flight and a 2.4/24 chance of getting the Los Angeles flight.

Using mathematics we can turn these probabilities into the following:

20/24 = 5/6, hence 5/6 of the thirty helpers, i.e. twenty-five people, arrive in Vegas.
1.6/24 = 2/30, hence two of the thirty helpers arrive in San Diego.
2.4/24 = 3/30, hence three of the thirty assistants arrive in Los Angeles.

Problem 15

The answer is both cunning and brilliant. In fact it is brilliantly cunning.

All 2,000 bottles are labelled. Each bottle has a unique combination of testers that have sampled it. If this combination of testers dies then the poisoned bottle will be known.

For simplicity, let's see how it would work in practice with sixteen bottles and four testers. We identify the testers as A, B, C and D, and a cross indicates that the testers drink from a particular bottle.

Bottle	Tester A	Tester B	Tester C	Tester D
1				
2	×			
3		×		
4	×	×		
5			×	
6	×		×	
7		×	×	
8	×	×	×	
9				×
10	×			×
11		×		×
12	×	×		×
13			×	×
14	×		×	×
15		×	×	×
16	×	×	×	×

From this grid we can see that if no testers die, then bottle one is the dodgy one. If tester C is the only tester to perish, then bottle number 5 was poisoned. If testers B and D both die then bottle 11 was dodgy. If, however, all four testers die then the bottle that all four sampled, bottle 16, was the poisoned one.

We can see that in order to work out how many different combinations can be covered by a set number of testers, all we have to do is to spot the emerging pattern in the table:

    1 tester – 1 combination
    2 testers – 4 combinations
    3 testers – 8 combinations
    4 testers – 16 combinations
    n testers – 2^n combinations

So all we have to do is extend the number of testers until they can cover up to 2,000 combinations, and all the bottles can be represented.

No. of testers	Total possible combinations
1	1
2	4
3	8
4	16
5	32
6	64

No. of testers	Total possible combinations
7	128
8	256
9	512
10	1,024
11	2,048

This means we need eleven testers to cover up to 2,000 bottles.

Izzittttt.

Problem 16

The toilet will only be electrified if it has been toggled an odd number of times, and this will only happen if the number of the toilet has an odd number of factors. Since factors have to be multiplied by other factors to make a number (e.g. $4 \times 6 = 24$, $8 \times 3 = 24$ etc.) factors always come in pairs. However, square numbers have one factor pair that is the factor multiplied by itself so it only counts as one factor.

Consider the number 36: 1×36, 2×18, 3×12, 4×9, 6×6.

Its factors are therefore 1 and 36, 2 and 18, 3 and 12, 4 and 9 and 6, giving a total of 9 factors, which is an odd number.

Square numbers are the only numbers that have an odd number of factors therefore their corresponding toilets are the only toilets that will be toggled an odd number of times and finish up electrified.

Therefore ten virgins will die – those on toilets 1, 4, 9, 16, 25, 36, 49, 64, 81, 100.

Problem 17

On the evening of the eightieth day all eighty wives kill their husbands.

Let's simplify the problem to only one wife and one husband. If everything else in the problem is the same, then the wife does not know that her husband is using a mobile phone. If Manchesterano lets slip that there is one mobile phone user in the village, she will know by default that it must be her own husband and will therefore be compelled to kill him.

What if there were two couples, each wife aware that the other wife's husband has a mobile. Manchesterano's revelation surprises neither wife, since each one thinks that the miscreant is the husband of the other. However, they will each think that the other wife knew of no mobile phone users until Manchesterano came along. They will each think, 'Now that Manchesterano's let the cat out of the bag, the other wife will surely work out that the malefactor must be her own husband'. Both wives know of only one offender, so they don't worry about their own husband. However, the next day arrives and no one is dead.

This is where it gets interesting. Each wife will work out that the other would have certainly killed her own husband unless she was already aware of a lawbreaker in the village. As the only candidate is their own husband, both wives realise that their own husbands are guilty and they are eliminated.

With three husbands and three wives, each of which knowing of two wrongdoers, nothing happens on the first day as expected but on the second day nothing happens either. Now each wife expected the murders to take place on the second day since they knew of two mobile phone users themselves. They therefore assumed that the other wives knew of only one transgressor each, since they could not know about their own.

Only on the third day, when no murders happened the night before do they realise that the other two wives must have already known of two errant husbands. Let's assume you are one of the wives. The other two couldn't have known anything about their own husbands' technological leanings, so the second wrongdoer they each knew about must have been your husband.

So the lack of action on the second night means that there must have been three villains in total and so the fallen husbands are all dispatched on the third evening.

This recursive reasoning continues in like fashion for any number of couples. In our case, with eighty wives and husbands, it works in the same way.

All wives know of seventy-nine deviant husbands, and therefore expect there to be seventy-nine eliminations on the seventy-ninth day. However dawn breaks and no CSI team is in the camp. There have been no murders and each wife is bitterly disappointed at discovering that their own husband must have been a technophile. 'The other seventy-nine, fine, but my own?'

So on the evening of the eightieth day, all husbands are slaughtered by their law-abiding wives.

Problem 18

As is fairly clear, the required strategy for the byguin to escape has to involve moving other than in a straight line otherwise Manny will be able to cover its moves. Therefore it starts heading off towards the edge but then instead of going straight to the water it begins to move in circles and gradually starts increasing their size.

As the circles start off fairly close to the centre, they have a small circumference, much less than a quarter of the circumference of the ice floe, and therefore Manny will gradually fall behind as he tries to track the byguin. What the byguin must do is to increase gradually the size of the circle it is travelling in to the maximum size at which Manchesterano is still falling behind.

As the byguin moves at one quarter of the speed of Manny, the circle that it travels in has to be just less than one

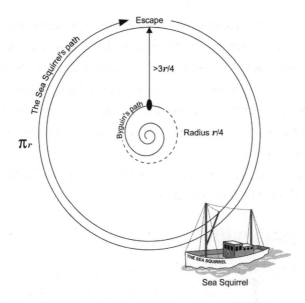

Figure 5 How the byguin escapes

quarter of the circumference. The circumference is $\pi \times$ diameter, $3.14 \times 30 = 94.2$ m, which divided by four is 23.55 m. If we round that down to 23.5 m to ensure that Manny slowly falls behind, then that leaves the byguin travelling in a circle with a circumference of 23.5 m and a radius of 3.74 m (circumference/π/2 = radius, i.e. $23.5/3.14/2 = 3.74$). As the byguin is travelling 3.74 m from the centre, that means it is now only 11.26 m from the safety of the water. Once Manchesterano is trailing the byguin by half a circumference of its circle, he will have to cover that distance ($94.2/2 = 47.1$ m) to capture the byguin should it make a dash for it. As the byguin is only 11.26 m away from the sea, it can now bolt across the floe into the water safe in the knowledge that Manny won't be able to get there before it, as $11.26 \times 4 = 45.04$ m, which is less than 47.1 m! Interesting, even if Manny and Erik had had the foresight to figure out that this is what the byguin was planning, there would be nothing they could have done about it. It seems that Erik truly underestimated the mental prowess of these elusive creatures.

Problem 19

The solution involves three steps:

1. Firstly, Gaston must encrypt the message and send it off to Jemima.
2. Then, upon receiving the email, Jemima must do something totally counter-intuitive: she encrypts the already encrypted message with her own key and sends it back to Gaston. Initially this doesn't seem to have helped at all; on top of not being able to read the message herself, Jemima has made things even trickier by adding her own encryption!
3. However, when Gaston receives the message back from Jemima (and this is the genius bit), he removes his own encryption, before sending the message on its final journey back to Jemima. On receiving the message for the second time, the only encryption preventing Jemima

from opening it is the one she added herself and therefore for which she possesses the decryption key. She can very easily remove this and happily read the message.

It might seem like a bit of a hassle since it requires three communications for every information exchange, but it is so secure that even if the CIA knows exactly what is being done, there is no way of intercepting any messages.

Still, it's a bit confusing in words, so here is a numerical example. Although we'll use a very short message and a very small prime number instead of a long message with a ridiculously gargantuan prime number.

OK, let's say Gaston wants to tell Jemima that the front door's security code is 9.

He encrypts the message by multiplying it by a prime number that only he knows, for example 7. Leaving him $9 \times 7 = 63$. He can now happily send this through the internet safe in the knowledge that the CIA will not be able to decrypt it. When it arrives at losamigosdelsoil@gmail. com, Jemima encrypts it further by multiplying it by another prime number: let's go with 13:

$13 \times 63 = 819$

She then sends this new message back to Gaston (still safe in the knowledge that the CIA can't crack it). On receiving it, Gaston removes his own encryption, by dividing by 7, which was his key:

$819/7 = 117$

He then sends it back one last time, at which point all Jemima needs to do is remove her own encryption by dividing by 13:

117/13

Which leaves them with 9 and the CIA truly stumped!

You may be asking, but how would Jemima know what was going on and that she is supposed to encrypt the message herself and send it back? Well, very simply, Gaston can tell her whatever he likes using no encryption whatsoever because even if the CIA knows what is happening, without knowing the actual prime numbers in question, there is nothing it can do about it. Bad one CIA.

Problem 20

The key is in realising that lamps do indeed give off something other than light: heat.

This gives a way of differentiating between lamps that are OFF and have never been ON and lamps that have been recently switched OFF.

The required strategy is to do the following to the switches in the control room:

Switch 1 – Leave OFF
Switch 2 – Turn ON
Switch 3 – Turn ON but switch OFF just as you leave the room to check on the light status.

When you then get to the lights you will be able to match up each light with the switches by inspecting the lights:

The light that is shining is controlled by Switch 2.

The light that is not shining and is also stone cold is controlled by Switch 1.

The light that is not shining but it still a little warm is controlled by Switch 3.

Then you can return to the control room and run the funk sequence knowing that you have identified the switches correctly.

Problem 21

The solution needs seven steps, so a bit of planning is required and working backwards is best.

Last step for the 8 litre container is to pour off 2 litres leaving 6 litres. Then all the other bits can be poured back into the 12 litre container leaving 6 litres in both 12 and 8 litre containers. We need to make a '2 space', so we can pour off 2 litres from a full 8 litre container. We can make a '2 space' by having 3 litres in the 5 litre container.

So we now need to get 3 litres. The difference between 8 and 5 is 3. That is the key.

So we fill up the 8 litre container and then fill the 5 litre from the 8 litre which leaves 3 litres in the 8 litre container.

We then empty the 5 litre container back into the 12 litre one and decant the 3 litres in the 8 litre container into the 5 litre one. We now have a '2 space' in the 5 litre container. We then fill the 8 litre container and then fill the '2 space' in the 5 litre container from the 8 litre container, leaving 6 litres. We empty the 5 litre container into the 12 litre container and we have 6 litres in each.

It's easier to follow in the table below, which shows the states of the containers after each step.

	12 litre	8 litre	5 litre
Start	12	0	0
Step 1	4 (12–8)	8	0
Step 2	4	3 (8-5)	5
Step 3	9 (4+5)	3	0
Step 4	9	0	3
Step 5	1 (9–8)	8	3
Step 6	1	6 (8–2)	5 (3 + 2)
Step 7	6 (1+5)	6	0

Problem 22

The first thing you should realise is that any pair takes as long as its slowest member. Therefore it makes sense to have the slowest two people going together. In this case it is Leon and Jean-Paul-Jean at five minutes and eight minutes respectively. They will still only take eight minutes to get across. Leon's slow speed of five minutes is not relevant as his slowness is 'used up' without increasing the overall time.

The next thing you must realise is that you cannot afford for either of this incredibly slow pair to make more than one journey. Therein lies the challenge. They have to go together but neither of them can bring back the torch.

That means they cannot start since one would have to bring back the torch and likewise they cannot end because one would be bringing back the torch to collect the last guy. That means they somehow have to go in the middle.

So Jemima and you must start taking a total of two minutes. It makes sense for the fastest person to go back with the torch; Jemima running back in one minute gives a total time of three minutes.

Now here is the stroke of genius. Jemima doesn't have to make the next journey!

There are three people waiting to cross of which any two can go. Since the slow guys must go as a pair, they go next taking eight minutes and leaving Jemima on her own. This brings the total time to eleven minutes.

Now we have three people who are safely across; You, Leon and Jean-Paul-Jean and Jemima on the other side still to cross back, and we have four minutes left.

So *you* are the one chosen to take the torch back as you are the fastest of the three on the other side. This takes two minutes and gives a total of thirteen minutes.

Now you and Jemima make the final crossing, which takes you both two minutes bringing the total time to fifteen minutes.

Problem 23

Firstly, the way to decrease the burn time of a fuse is to burn it at both ends. This will cut the burn time in half. This means that you now have the capacity to identify a thirty-second period of time with one fuse and a sixty-second period with the other.

Having more than one match means that you can light these fuses at different times too. In fact the solution is to light one fuse at one end and the other at both ends. Let's call them Fuse A and Fuse B:

Fuse A has been lit at one end only – it will take sixty seconds to burn through.
Fuse B has been lit at both ends – it will take thirty seconds to burn through.

The trick here now is to watch both fuses closely and when Fuse B has burnt through, you light the other end of Fuse A.

Fuse A had thirty seconds to burn through before you lit its other end, so now it will burn the rest of it through at twice the speed – i.e. burn through in fifteen seconds.

This gives you the forty-five seconds you need.

The most elegant way of doing it is like this:

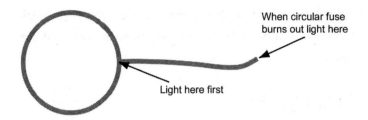

Figure 6 How to light the fuses

Arrange one fuse in a circle and one in a straight line. Light the point at which the circle meets the straight fuse first and both fuses will start burning. When the circular fuse has burnt through, light the other end of the straight fuse as shown in Figure 6.

Problem 24

I like the solution to this one a lot. It's very simple but quite brilliant.

The following steps are taken:

1. Start both hourglasses at the same time.
2. When the five-hour finishes, flip it over.

Five hours have passed, so there are three hours remaining in the eight-hour one. This means that when the eight-hour one has finished, (after eight hours), three hours of sand has passed through the five-hour one. If the five-hour is flipped at this point, there will be three hours worth of sand to run back out leading to a total of eleven hours.

Time	Eight-hour	Five-hour
0	Starts	Starts
5		Finishes – flip
8	Finishes	Flip again
11		Finishes

There is another way of doing this that involves a bit of time wastage at the beginning. It's good, but this solution is better.

Problem 25

Let's go over the basic facts:

The armies are twenty miles apart.

Merlin rides at 30 mph.

Ghengis's Army travels at 11 mph.

Richard's Army travels at 4 mph.

The first thing is to work out the relative speed of the armies: 11 + 4 = 15 mph

This means that they are getting closer at a rate of 15 mph. Since they start twenty miles apart, they will meet in one hour and twenty minutes.

This means that Merlin's journey time is also one hour and twenty minutes. Since Merlin rides at 30 mph, he will travel a distance of forty miles. Or, more simply, as Merlin's speed is double that of the combined armies he will travel twice as far.

There is a maths answer as well, to do with summing an infinite series. Google it if you like: 'fly problem von Neumann'.

Problem 26

This is best solved by reducing to the simplest possible case and then extrapolating step by step with the inclusion of some sort of signalling system. Of course the signalling system can have no indication of the hat colour of any individual.

In the simplest possible case there are two people. Each can see the other's hat. One will only see blue and rightly deduce that his own hat is red and will stand up since there is at least one hat of each colour.

We then consider the next simplest case: that of three people. Let's imagine there are two red hats and one blue hat. Each knight with a red hat can see one red and one blue.

If I can see a red and a blue and I have a blue myself, the other red hatted knight will immediately stand up as he can only see blue hats. However, since he can see one red and one blue he will not stand up. This is the secret! Non action gives information.

I correctly deduce that since he does not stand up he cannot work out the colour of his own hat. This means that he must be able to see another red hat and so I deduce that I am wearing red.

This logic applies to both knights wearing the red hats. If no one stands up immediately then both red hatted knights will stand up after a while.

The key to a successful strategy therefore is to link the stand-up times to regular intervals of time. Therefore if you cannot see any red hats, you stand up after one minute. If you can see only one red hat and that knight does not stand up after one minute, you stand up after two minutes and so on.

Roll it forward a little. You can see seventeen red hats.

Let's see what would happen if you had a blue hat:

Each knight wearing a red hat can see only sixteen red hats. Therefore these knights all stand up on the seventeenth minute.

However, if you had a red hat, there are now eighteen hats but you can only see seventeen of them and everyone with a red hat would see seventeen red hats. So nothing would happen after the seventeenth minute. Anyone who can see seventeen red hats stands up on the eighteenth minute.

This all sounds pretty complicated but it can be summed up in a simple strategy: 'Stand up one minute after the number of red hats you can see'. So if you see three red hats, stand up on the fourth minute. If you see nine red hats, stand up on the tenth minute.

But what if I am wearing a blue hat I hear you cry? What if I stand up thinking I am wearing red and I am actually wearing blue? What if I can see seven red hats, I stand up on the eighth minute and I blow the whole thing?

If you have a blue hat then anyone wearing a red hat will only see six red hats and so they will all stand up on the seventh minute. There will be no eighth minute!

However the strategy will still work. You will have seen all the red hats get up after minute seven, so you will be standing up on minute eight along with all the blue hat wearers and you will all know your hat colour by then.

Problem 27

This is a beauty this one. The first realisation is that there will be three single links from your three breaks in the chain. So this takes care of the first three kills.

Thinking ahead and doing a thought experiment you realise that for the fourth kill you will have a problem: You know instinctively that you must need bigger pieces from somewhere since you are only making three breaks, but you are not sure exactly how many links you're going to need in these bigger pieces.

Since it is a net increase of one link per kill you can take back the three links you've already parted with and replace them with a four-link piece.

This means that the first break in the chain must be on the fifth link.

This would leave you with a four-link piece, the broken link and the fifty-eight-link rest of the chain, as shown in Figure 7.

Figure 7 The first break in the chain

So, you then carry on going kill by kill, visualising what would happen until the eighth day. Now you need to be able to take back the four-link piece and the three single links and replace them all with an eight-link piece.

So you need to break the fifty-eight-link piece on the ninth link leaving an eight-link piece, a single link and a forty-nine-link piece.

Notice the pattern? It's our old friend Baron Binary.

You then continue your thought experiment and realise that the next large piece you will need is a sixteen-link piece. So the forty-nine-link piece needs to be broken at the seventeenth link which will leave the sixteen-link piece, the single link and the final piece of the chain which now has thirty-two links left in it. Symmetry in motion. In this way you can carry on going all the way to sixty-three pieces through swapping backwards and forwards as before.

Nice.

Figure 8 The second break in the chain

Problem 28

Genghis cannot be left alone with either of the other two so he must be taken first. Peter then returns to collect Richard or Mary, it matters not which of them he takes. Let's say it was Richard.

So he takes Richard over but the dilemma is that he can't leave Richard and Genghis alone when he goes back to get Mary. Here's the genius – he leaves Richard but takes Genghis back in the boat!

Peter then drops Genghis back where he started and collects Mary. He then drops Mary off before returning to get Genghis and take him over for the second time.

Problem 29

In order to escape, the team have to 'fight fire with fire' and act totally counter-intuitively. In fact the best strategy is to light a series of fires in a line across the island, downwind of the current fire and perpendicular to the direction of the wind.

There will now be two lines of fire both moving in the same direction, the direction the wind is blowing, either side of our heroes. They can then walk in the path of the fire that they just created, following the charred path as it burns through the rest of the island.

When the original fire reaches the patch of land where they started their own fire, all the vegetation will have already been burnt. The fire will have nothing to sustain it

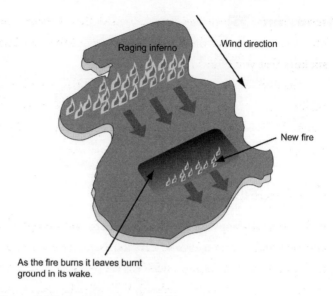

Raging inferno

Wind direction

New fire

As the fire burns it leaves burnt ground in its wake.

Figure 9 How to escape a raging inferno

and it will die out. Our protagonists survive the first Mucho Pollo death trap.

Problem 30

The first thing most people do is see what happens if you divide the eight keys into two halves. Pretty soon it becomes obvious that this strategy is found wanting as it requires that the weighing balance is used three times.

The trick to this problem is to realise that you can discover information about a key without actually weighing it. Since the correct key is very slightly heavier than the other seven, if you choose any two keys and they balance each other, you know that the heavier key is one of the remaining six keys that you didn't put on the balance.

The correct strategy is to divide the eight keys into three smaller groups: three, three and two. The first step is to weigh the two groups of three keys against each other. There are two possible results: balanced or unbalanced.

If unbalanced

If the weighing apparatus is unbalanced, it will be tipped to one side and you can deduce that the correct key is one of the three keys on the lower side. You can then weigh any two of those three keys against each other. If on doing this the pans are level, then the heavy key must be the third. If they are not level, then you'll easily be able to see which key is heavier.

If balanced

If however, the apparatus is level, you know that the correct key must be one of the two keys you didn't weigh. You can easily weigh them and find out which one it is.

Problem 31

Currently you have two Killabasten pills and one Sharkenkampf pill which are all identical and the correct dose is one pill of each. The trick is to realise that you need to even up the score a little and take out one more Sharkenkampf pill. This seems counter-intuitive since we already have too many pills, but the solution is quite elegant.

In fact there are actually two solutions from hereon in.

The first involves grinding all the pills up and creating a big pile of powder that is 50% Killabasten and 50% Sharkenkampf. Then, when it has all been mixed up perfectly, you can divide the pile in half and take half now and half when the next dose is required in an hour's time.

The second solution involves cutting all the four pills you now have into eight halves. Since you do not know exactly which pill is which out of the three original pills you might think it is a bit of a problem, however, with the addition of the second S pill it now makes no difference. It may make sense to see it drawn out:

Half 1	Half 2
K or S	K or S
K or S	K or S
K or S	K or S
S	S

The realisation is that it doesn't matter which pill is Killabasten and which is Sharkenkampf out of the first three you had. As soon as you have added another Sharkenkampf to the mix and then cut the pills in half, you will be taking a total dose of exactly one Killabasten and one Sharkenkampf whenever you take the four half pills.

You take all the parts in *Half 1* and save *Half 2* for next time you need to escape a gassy death.

Well done, you stay alive another 900 years … or do you?

Problem 32

The gang must use the fish in the boat to lure one of the biggest sharks into the boat.

Unlikely, yes. Impractical, almost certainly. Theoretically possible, that's why it's the answer.

Since sharks have no swim bladder they are actually denser than water – they sink if they stop moving (look it up – www.sharksaredenserthanwater.com). Since they are denser than water, they are only displacing an amount of water equal to their volume when swimming in the lake. However, once lured into the boat, the shark's weight is now supported by the boat and provided the boat doesn't now sink (it doesn't), the shark's weight is therefore supported by the water. A floating object displaces an amount of water equal to its weight, thus the shark when in the boat displaces more water than when submerged.

As more water is now displaced, the water level rises, triggering the sensors and the blast doors are opened. Once again our statistically impossible protagonists have managed to thwart their foes.

So you think you're clever?

If you've calculated, considered or even cheated your way through the *Electric Toilet Virgin Death Lottery* puzzles, you'll have noticed that the fiendish final puzzle doesn't have a solution provided. You'll have to apply your already addled mind to finishing it yourself. But it will be worth it for one lucky winner* plucked from the genii who submit the correct answer. They will be rewarded with a grand prize of one grand (£1000). And that's not all! Once they've won the cash, they should make the most of it, because that man or woman will also get the chance to be sacrificed as a character in the forthcoming sequel!

To apply, send your completed solution and working either by email to **info@oneworld-publications.com** with the words "Toilet Competition" in the subject line, or to Virgin Death Lottery, 185 Banbury Road, Oxford, OX2 7AR.

The correct entries will be entered into a prize draw, and the winner will be contacted within seven days of the closing date.

Closing date: 31 May 2010

*Terms and conditions apply

Terms and Conditions